A SOLDIER OF THE
Seventy-first

D1375988

*'Enthralling account by an unknown Highland Light infantryman
of his part in the Napoleonic Wars'*

The Good Book Guide

*'The author was a lettered Edinburgh lad known only as Tom. He
joined up in 1806 on the spur of the moment and was often to regret it
over nine years of hunger, exposure and fatigue, sometimes marching
40 miles in a day without shoes. The wonder is that he and his
companions were able time and again, after giving three cheers, to rout
the French and "put them to the right-about". By Waterloo – his last
and noisiest battle – he was inured to the misery he saw all around him,
but preserved to the end his sense of compassion for individual
suffering. His elegant style and his descriptive power take us with him
at every step.'*

The Sunday Telegraph

Other Military Books published by The Windrush Press

The Recollections of Rifleman Harris
Edited and Introduced by Christopher Hibbert

The Letters of Private Wheeler
Edited and with a Foreword by B. H. Liddell Hart

The Diaries of a Napoleonic Foot Soldier
Edited and Introduced by Mark Raeff

GREAT BATTLE SERIES

Hastings
Peter Poyntz Wright

Agincourt
Christopher Hibbert

Edgehill: 1642
Peter Young

Corunna
Christopher Hibbert

Wellington's Peninsular Victories
Michael Glover

Waterloo: A Near Run Thing
David Howarth

Trafalgar: The Nelson Touch
David Howarth

A SOLDIER OF THE
Seventy-first

THE JOURNAL OF A SOLDIER IN THE PENINSULAR WAR

∎

EDITED AND INTRODUCED BY

CHRISTOPHER HIBBERT

THE WINDRUSH PRESS · GLOUCESTERSHIRE

This edition first published in Great Britain
by Leo Cooper Limited in 1975
Reprinted in 1996 and 1997 by The Windrush Press
Little Window, High Street,
Moreton-in-Marsh,
Gloucestershire GL56 0LL
Telephone: 01608 652012
Fax: 01608 652125

ISBN 0 900075 89 9

The painting on the front cover is 'Battle of Vimiera, 21 August 1808:
The Bravery of the Scotch Piper Steward of the
71st Highland Regiment'.
© The Trustees of the National Museums of Scotland 1996.

Printed and bound in Great Britain by
The Lavenham Press Ltd., Suffolk

ACKNOWLEDGEMENT

The editor and publishers would like to express their gratitude to E. J. Webb who first suggested that this book should be reprinted.

Since this book was reprinted in 1975, new evidence has come to light which suggests that the author of the journal was a certain Thomas Howell. Nothing more is known of him. However, a note on the fly-leaf of a first (1819) edition, then owned by David Dundas Scott and now in the possession of Mr Rex Doublet, states that Scott met a soldier from Fife called John Mitchell, who also served in the 71st, in 1852. During their conversation, Mitchell 'confirmed in the fullest manner the admirably related statements of this book'.
The publishers are grateful to Rex Doublet for bringing this tantalising piece of information to their attention.

CONTENTS

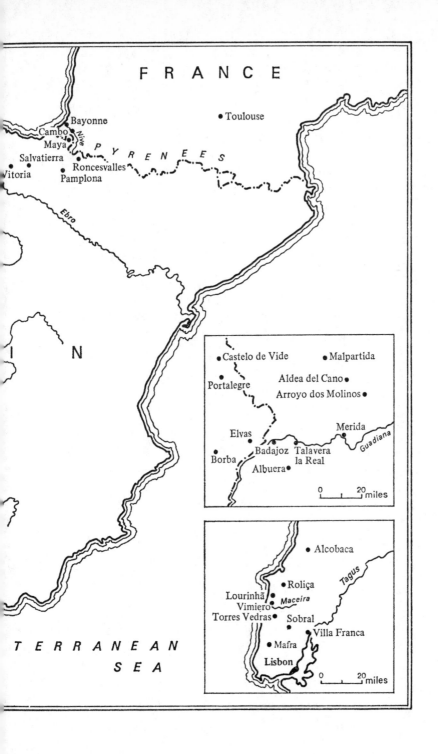

Introduction

Readers of books about Wellington's army have long been familiar with the anonymous soldier of the 71st Highlanders whose vivid record of his experiences has enlivened so many narratives of the Peninsular War. Yet the journal from which military historians have so often quoted has been out of print for so many years and, in its entirety, has been known only to the specialist. It deserves a far wider readership than it has previously enjoyed.

Unlike most other soldiers' memoirs of the period it covers the whole of the Peninsular War from the landing in Mondego Bay in August, 1808, to the defeat of the French at Vitoria in 1813. It opens with a rare description of that inglorious campaign in South America in 1806. It includes a disturbing account of the ill-fated expedition to Walcheren where the author contracted the fever that killed four thousand of his comrades and rendered his fellow-memoirist, Rifleman Harris, unfit for further duty. And it ends at Waterloo where he narrowly escaped death when a cannon-ball struck the ground in front of him, knocked him head over heels and shattered his musket.

In Belgium as in Spain, in Germany as in Uruguay, the author's sharp eye for the illuminating detail and the oddities

of human behaviour enabled him to present a picture of
army life as graphic and revealing as any drawn by a private
soldier during the Napoleonic Wars. We are given unfor-
gettable glimpses of stragglers tramping through the blood-
spattered snow on the dreadful retreat to Corunna; of soldiers
charging into battle through the smoke, and lying down in
the open fields to sleep at night, their hair frozen to the
ground by morning, their shoulders black with bruises from
the recoil of their muskets. We are told of vultures swooping
down upon the fields of dead, seeming to fight with the
burial parties for possession of the bodies; of Portuguese
peasants killing and robbing the wounded, and then, as
darkness falls, lighting great fires around which they sit all
night 'shouting like as many savages'. We see a young officer
in action for the first time, nervously running backwards
and forwards as if trying to escape the shot and shell until
calmed by an old soldier who says to him, 'with all the
gravity of a Turk, "You need not hide, Sir. If there is
any thing there for you it will find you out".' We hear other
officers, hardened by war, restraining their men as they
advance together in line, calmly repeating, ' "Steady, lads,
steady!" and that in an undertone.' We share the author's
horror when a flicker of candlelight reveals that the huge
cask from which he has been drinking wine in a dark
Spanish store contains the corpse of an enemy soldier. We
feel his queasiness when one of his comrades cooks and
eats a human arm and declares it 'very sweet'. We pity him
when, exhausted and hungry, he is sent to make a mess of
broken biscuit for Lord Wellington's hounds and has his
'own fill—a thing I had not got for some days'. And we,
too, are relieved when, knocked down by a spent shot which
strikes him in the groin and makes him feel sick, his life is

spared by a French soldier who, instead of bayoneting him, gives him a pancake out of his hat.

There are many pleasant moments such as this. And when we put the book down it is not only the horrors of war which we remember, but English soldiers eating sausages and dancing to a French band during a truce; a French general ludicrously angry in defeat, gnashing his teeth and jumping up and down on his cocked hat; and the colonel of the 71st, upbraiding his men for stealing flour from a mill, induced to join in their laughter as a hen he has looted himself suddenly pops its head out of his coat pocket.

In recalling these incidents I hope I have been able to convey something of the flavour of the book and to whet your appetite for the pages that follow. To make these pages easier to read the punctuation has been modified and where the sense is, on first reading, rather obscure I have added a word or a phrase and placed it in square brackets. My own explanations and interpolations are in italics. Otherwise— apart from correcting misspelling of proper names—I have not tampered with the original text which is here printed in full, except for a few rather tedious paragraphs whose gist is given below or in the prefaces to the ensuing chapters.

A few notes have been included, mainly to elucidate obscure references or to provide information about the various senior officers to whom the author refers. And I have added an appendix which gives the present titles of regiments mentioned in the text. But no attempt has been made to widen the scope of what is essentially a personal narrative. For their help with some of the notes I am grateful to Major F. W. Myatt, M.C., and Major-General B. P. Hughes, C.B., C.B.E.

The full title of the book is JOURNAL OF A SOLDIER OF THE 71ST OR GLASGOW REGIMENT, HIGHLAND LIGHT INFANTRY

FROM *1806 to 1815.* I have not been able to trace a copy of the first edition which is not known either to the British Museum, the National Library of Scotland, the National Army Museum or the Ministry of Defence Library. It probably first appeared as a serial in some periodical. The second edition—upon which this one is based—was published in Edinburgh in 1819. It was reprinted in 1822, 1828 and in 1835.

The author, who 'from motives of delicacy', chose to conceal his surname—his Christian name was Thomas—was born in Edinburgh in 1790. 'It was their ambition to educate me for one of the learned professions,' he writes of his 'poor but respectable parents', 'my mother wishing me to be a clergyman, my father, to be a writer. They kept from themselves many comforts that I might appear genteel and attend the best schools. My brothers and sister did not appear to belong to the same family. My parents had three children, two boys and a girl, besides myself. On me alone was lavished all their care. My brothers, John and William, could read and write and, at the age of twelve years, were bound apprentices to trades. My sister, Jane, was made, at home, a servant-of-all-work to assist my mother. I alone was a gentleman in a house of poverty.'

The family income was no more than 11s a week, 5s being contributed by Thomas's two brothers, the other 6s coming from a benefit society as their father's poor state of health prevented him from working. Resenting the poverty which drew a sharp distinction between himself and the other boys at his school, Thomas became sullen and quarrelsome. He abandoned his studies, and, at the age of sixteen, decided to become an actor. 'Tall and well made, of a genteel appearance and address', he had every confidence in his success when the manager of the Edinburgh theatre offered him an audition. His parents pleaded with him not to go; but.

ignoring their tearful entreaties, he stormed out of the house. Once on the stage, however, his confidence deserted him.

'I trembled', he recorded. 'A cold sweat oozed through every pore; my father's and mother's words rung in my ears; my senses became confused; hisses began from the audience; I utterly failed . . . I shrank unseen from the theatre, bewildered and in a state of despair. I wandered the whole night. In the morning early, meeting a party of recruits about to embark, I rashly offered to go with them. My offer was accepted and I embarked at Leith, with seventeen others, for the Isle of Wight in July, 1806.'

On arrival at Newport he enlisted for seven years in the 71st (Highland) Regiment of Foot and received a bounty of eleven guineas. Keeping four pounds for himself, he sent the remainder to his parents with a letter of the most heartfelt contrition.

'Now I began to drink the cup of bitterness,' he continued. 'How different was my situation from what it had been! Forced from bed at five o'clock each morning, to get all things ready for drill; then drilled for three hours with the most unfeeling rigour, and often beat by the sergeant for the faults of others. I who had never been crossed at home, I who never knew fatigue, was now fainting under it . . . I could not associate with the common soldiers; their habits made me shudder. I feared an oath—they never spoke without one: I could not drink—they loved liquor: They gamed—I knew nothing of play. Thus was I a solitary individual among hundreds. They lost no opportunity of teasing me. "Saucy Tom," or "The distressed Methodist,"*

*Methodist was a soldier's term for any quiet, reserved, abstemious comrade and did not necessarily have a religious connotation, though there *were* many Methodists in the Army on which their influence was considerable.

were the names they distinguished me by. I had no way of redress until an event occurred that gave me, against my will, an opportunity to prove that my spirit was above insult.

'A recruit who had joined at the same time with myself was particularly active in his endeavours to turn me into ridicule. One evening I was sitting in a side-window, reading. Of an old newspaper he made a fool's cap, and, unperceived by me, placed it upon my head. Fired at the insult, I started up and knocked him down. "Clear the room; a ring, a ring,—the Methodist is going to fight," was vociferated from all sides. Repenting my haste, yet determined not to affront myself, I stood firm and determined to do my utmost. My antagonist, stunned by the violence of the blow and surprised at the spirit I displayed, rose slowly and stood irresolute. I demanded an apology. He began to bluster and threaten, but I saw at once that he was afraid; and turning from him, said, in a cool decided manner, "If you dare again insult me, I will chastise you as you deserve; you are beneath my anger." I again sat down, and resumed my reading, as if nothing had happened.

'From this time I was no longer insulted; and I became much esteemed among my fellow-soldiers, who before despised me. Still, I could not associate with them. Their pleasures were repugnant to my feelings.'

Fifteen days after his arrival in the Isle of Wight, and before he had received an answer from his parents, the author was ordered to embark for the Cape of Good Hope where his regiment was to garrison the recently captured colony. But he had been there less than three weeks when the 71st received orders to embark once more, this time for South America where, in June, 1806, a British force of about 1,500 men under Colonel William Carr Beresford had made a bold attack upon the Spaniards and had captured Buenos Aires. It was hoped that by reinforcing Beresford's small army, its initial success would be exploited and a new channel opened up for British trade.

CHRISTOPHER HIBBERT

I

South America
1806-1807

WE ARRIVED in the River Plate in October, 1806, when we were informed that the Spaniards had retaken Buenos Aires [and captured Colonel Beresford] and that our troops only possessed Maldonado, a small space [at the mouth of the river about sixty miles east of Montevideo]. On our disembarkation, we found the remains of the army in the greatest want of every necessary belonging to an army and quite disheartened. On the land side they were surrounded by about 400 horsemen who cut off all their foraging parties and intercepted all supplies. These horsemen were not regular soldiers, but the inhabitants of the country who had turned out to defend their homes from the enemy.

Soon after our arrival at Maldonado, the Spaniards advanced out of Montevideo to attack us. They were about 600, and had, besides, a number of great guns with them. They came upon us in two columns, the right consisting of cavalry, the left of infantry, and bore so hard upon our out-picquet of 400 men that Colonel Brown, who commanded our left, ordered Major Campbell, with three companies of the 40th regiment, to its support. These charged the head of the column. The Spaniards stood firm and fought bravely; numbers fell on both sides; but the gallant 40th drove them back with the point of the bayonet. Sir Samuel Auchmuty[1] ordered the rifle corps and light battalion to attack the rear of their column, which was done with the utmost spirit. Three cheers were the signal of our onset. The Spaniards fled, and the right column, seeing the fate of their left, set spurs to their horses and fled, without having shared in the action. There remained in our possession one General and a great number of prisoners, besides one of their great guns. They left about 300 dead on the field. We had very few wounded prisoners, and these were taken in the pursuit. I saw them carry their people back to the town, as soon as they were hurt. Our loss was much less than theirs.

After this action, we saw no more of our troublesome guests, the horsemen, who used to brave us in our lines and even wound our people in the camp.

This was the first blood I had ever seen shed in battle; the first time the cannon had roared in my hearing, charged with death. I was not yet seventeen years of age, and had not been six months from home. My limbs bending under me with fatigue, in a sultry clime, the musket and accoutrements that I was forced to carry were insupportably oppressive. Still I bore all with invincible patience. During the action, the thought of death never once crossed my mind. After the firing commenced, a still sensation stole over my whole frame, a firm determined torpor, bordering on insensibility. I heard an old soldier answer, to a youth like myself, who inquired what he should do during the battle, 'Do your duty'.

As the battalion to which I belonged returned from the pursuit, we passed, in our way to the camp, over the field of the dead. It was too much for my feelings; I was obliged to turn aside my head from the horrid sight. The birds of prey seemed to contend with those who were burying the slain for the possession of the bodies. Horrid sight! Men who in the morning, exulting, trod forth in strength; whose minds, only fettered by their bodies, seemed to feel restraint, now lay shockingly mangled and a prey to animals: and *I* had been an assistant in this work of death! I almost wished I had been a victim.

Until the 2nd of November, my fatigue was great. Constructing batteries and other works, we were forced to labour night and day. My hands, when I left home, were white and soft; now they were excoriated and brown and, where they were unbroken, as hard as horn. Often overpowered by fatigue, sleep has sealed my eyes; I have awoke groaning with thirst, and the intense heat of my hands. It was then I felt, in all its horror, the folly of my former conduct. Bitter was the sigh that acknowledged my punishment was just.

In the storming of Montevideo, I had no share. We remained with the camp to protect the rear. While we lay before the town, the shells of the enemy were falling, often near where I stood; one, in particular, seemed as if it would fall at our feet. A young officer ran backwards and forwards, as if he would hide himself; an old soldier said to him, with all the gravity of a Turk, 'You need not hide, Sir; if there is any thing there for you, it will find you out.' The young man looked confused, stood to his duty, and I never saw him appear uneasy again: so soon was he converted to the warrior's doctrine.

We marched into Montevideo, the day after the assault, where I remained seven months. It is a most delightful country, were it not so hot. The evening is the only tolerable time of the day. The sea breeze sets in about eight or nine o'clock in the morning, which mitigates the heat a good deal; yet I suffered much. It was now the middle of December. Summer had commenced with all its sweets, on a scale I had no conception of; neither can I convey any idea of it in words. We had the greatest abundance of every article of food and, as the summer advanced, the choicest fruit; indeed, even more than we could consume, and at length we loathed it.

I had been, along with the other youths, appointed to Sir Samuel Auchmuty's guard, as the least fatiguing duty. I would have been comparatively happy had I known my parents were well and had pardoned me. The uncertainty of this, and reflections on my past conduct, kept me in a state of continual gloom.

I was billeted upon a young widow who did all in her power to make me comfortable, alongside with her aged father. Her husband had been slain in the first attack of our troops upon the place and she remained inconsolable. During the seven months I remained in Montevideo she behaved to me like a mother. To her I was indebted for many comforts. Never shall I forget Maria de Parides. She was of a small figure, yet elegant in her appearance. Like the other women of the country, she was very brown; her eyes sparkling, black as jet; her teeth equal and white. She wore her own hair, when dressed, as is the fashion of the country, in plaits down her back. It was very long and of glossy black. Her dress was very plain: a black veil covered her head, and her mantilla was tied, in the most graceful manner, under her chin. This was the common dress of all the women; the only difference was in the colour of their mantillas and shoes. These they often wore of all colours, and sometimes the veil was white. The men wore the cloak and hat of the Spaniards, but many of them had sandals, and a great many wanted both shoes and stockings.

The native women were the most uncomely I ever beheld. They have broad noses, thick lips, and are of very small stature. Their hair, which is long, black and hard to the feel, they wear frizzled up in front in the most hideous manner, while it hangs down their backs below the waist. When they dress, they stick in it feathers and flowers, and walk about in all the pride of ugliness. The men are short of stature, stout made, and have large joints. They are brave, but indolent to excess. I have seen them galloping about on horseback, almost naked, with silver spurs on their bare heels, perhaps an old rug upon their shoulders. They fear not pain. I have seen them with hurts ghastly to look at, yet they never seemed to mind them. As for their idleness, I have seen them lie stretched, for a whole day, gazing upon the river, and their wives bring them their victuals; and, if they were not pleased with the quantity, they would beat them furiously. This is the only exertion they ever make readily—venting their fury upon their wives. They prefer flesh to any other food, and they eat it almost raw, and in quantities which a European would think impossible.

I had little opportunity of seeing the best sort of Spanish settlers, as they had all left the place before we took it; and, during the siege, those I had any opportunity of knowing were of the poorer sort, who used to visit Maria de Parides and her father, Don Santanos. They are ignorant in the extreme and very superstitious. Maria told me, with the utmost concern, that the cause of her husband's death was his being bewitched by an old

Indian, to whom he had refused some partridges as he returned from hunting a few days before the battle.

As I became acquainted with the language, I observed many singular traits of character. When Maria or old Santanos yawned they crossed their mouth with the utmost haste to prevent the Devil going down their throats. If Santanos sneezed, Maria called, '*Jesus!*' his answer was, '*Muchas gracias,*' 'Many thanks.' When they knock at any door, they say, '*Ave Maria purissima*'; they open at once, as they think no one with an evil intent will use this holy phrase. When they meet a woman, they say '*A sus pies senora*' or '*Beso los pies de Usted*'— 'I lay myself at your feet' or 'I kiss your feet.' As they part, he says, '*Me tengo a sus pies de Usted*' or '*Baxo de sus pies*'—'I am at your feet' or 'Keep me at your feet.' She replies '*Beso a Usted la mano, Cavallero*'—'I kiss your hand, Sir.' When they leave anyone they say '*Vaya Usted con Díos*' or '*Con la Virgen*'—'May God (or the Holy Virgin) attend you.' When they are angry, it is a common phrase with them, '*Vaya Usted con cien mil Demonios*'—'Begone with a hundred thousand devils.'

Maria was concerned that I should be a heretic and wished much I would change my religion and become a Catholic, as the only means of my salvation. In vain I said to her, '*Muchos caminos al cielo*'—'Many roads to Heaven.' There were few priests in the town, as they had thought it better to move off to Buenos Aires with the church plate etc before we took the town than trust to their prayers and our generosity. Maria, however, got one to convert me, as her own father-confessor had gone with the rest. It was in the afternoon, on my return from guard, I first met him. His appearance made an impression on me much in his favour. He was tall and graceful, and

wore his beard, which was grey and full, giving a vener-
able cast to his face, and softening the wrinkles that time
had made in his forehead. Maria introduced me to him,
as a young man who was willing to receive instruction
and one she wished much to believe in all the doctrines
of the Holy Church, that I might not be lost forever
through my unbelief. He then began to say a great deal
about the errors of the protestants, and their undone
state, since they had left the true church. The only
answer I made was 'Muchos caminos al cielo.' He shook
his head and said all heretics were a stubborn sort of
people, but begged me to consider of what he said. I
answered, certainly I would; and we parted friends.
Maria was much disappointed at my not being convinced
at once and her father, Santanos, said he had no doubt
that I would yet become a good Catholic and remain with
them. I loved them the more for their disinterested zeal.
Their only wish was for my welfare.

Thus had I passed my time, until the arrival of
General Whitelocke with reinforcements in the beginning
of May, 1807.[2] It was the middle of winter at Montevideo; the nights were frosty, with now and then a little
snow, and great showers of hail as large as beans. In
the day dreadful rains deluged all around. We had sometimes thunder and lightning. One night in particular the
whole earth seemed one continued blaze. The mountain
on the side of which the town is built re-echoed the
thunder, as if it would rend in pieces. The whole inhabitants flocked to the churches or kneeled in the streets.

On the arrival of the reinforcements, we were formed
into a brigade, alongside with the light companies of the
36th, 38th, 40th, 87th, and four companies of the 95th
regiments. On the 28th June, we assembled near Ensenada

de Barragon with the whole army and commenced our march towards Buenos Aires.

The country is almost all level and covered with long clover that reached to our waists, and large herds of bullocks and horses which seemed to run wild. The weather was very wet. For days I had not a dry article on my body. We crossed many morasses in our march, in one of which I lost my shoes and was under the necessity of marching the rest of the way barefooted. We passed the river at a ford called Passorico, under the command of Major-General Gower.[3] Here, we drove back a body of the enemy. We were, next day, joined by General Whitelocke and the remainder of the army. Upon his joining us, the line was formed by Sir Samuel Auchmuty on the left, stretching towards a convent called the Recolletta, distant from the left about two miles. Two regiments were stationed on the right. Brigadier-General Craufurd's[4] brigade occupied the centre and possessed the principal avenues to the town, which was distant from the great square and fort three miles. Three regiments extended towards the Residenta on the right.

The town and suburbs are built in squares of about 140 yards on each side; and all the houses are flat on the top for the use of the inhabitants, who go upon them to enjoy the cool of the evening. These, we were told, they meant to occupy with their slaves and fire down upon us as we charged through the streets. From the disposition of our army, the town was nearly surrounded.

We remained under arms on the morning of the 5th of July, waiting the order to advance. Judge our astonishment when the word was given to march without ammunition, with fixed bayonets only. 'We are betrayed,' was whispered through the ranks. 'Mind your duty, my lads; onwards, onwards, Britain for ever,' were the last words I heard our noble Captain Brookman utter. He fell as we entered the town. Onwards we rushed, carrying every thing before us, scrambling over ditches and other impediments which the inhabitants had placed in our way. At the corner of every street, and flanking all the ditches, they had placed cannon that thinned our ranks every step we took. Still onwards we drove, up one street, down another, until we came to the church of St Domingo, where the colours of the 71st Regiment had been placed as a trophy over the shrine of the Virgin Mary. We made a sally into it, and took them from that disgraceful resting place, where they had remained ever since the surrender of General Beresford[5] to General Liniers.[6] Now we were going to sally out in triumph. The Spaniards had not been idle. The entrances of the church were barricaded, and cannon placed at each entrance. We were forced to surrender and were marched to prison. It was there I first learned the complete failure of our enterprise.

During the time we were charging through the streets many of our men made sallies into the houses in search of plunder; and many were encumbered with it at the time of our surrender. One serjeant of the 38th had made a longish hole in his wooden canteen, like that over the money drawer in the counter of a retail shop; into it he slipped all the money he could lay his hands upon. As he came out of a house he had been ransacking, he was shot through the head. In his fall the canteen burst and a great many doubloons ran in all directions on the street. Then commenced a scramble for

the money and about eighteen men were shot, grasping
at the gold they were never to enjoy. They even snatched
it from their dying companions, although they themselves were to be in the same situation the next moment.

We were all searched and every article that was
Spanish taken from us, but we were allowed to keep the
rest. During the search one soldier, who had a good many
doubloons, put them into his camp-kettle, with flesh and
water above them, placed all upon a fire and kept them
safe.

There were about one hundred of us, who had been
taken in the church, marched out of prison to be shot,
unless we produced a gold crucifix of great value, that
was missing. We stood in a large circle of Spaniards and
Indians. Their levelled pieces and savage looks gave us
little hope unless the crucifix was produced. It was found
on the ground, on the spot where we stood; but it was
not known who had taken it. The troops retired, and we
were allowed to go back to prison without further
molestation.

Four days after we were made prisoners, the good
priest I had conversed with in the house of Maria de
Parides, came to me in prison, and offered to obtain my
release if I would only say that I would, at any future
time, embrace the Catholic faith. He held out many in-
ducements. I thanked him kindly for his offer, but told
him it was impossible I ever could. He said, 'I have done
my duty, as a servant of God; now I will do it, as a man.'
He never again spoke to me of changing my religion,
yet he visited me every day with some comfort or
another.

Donald M'Donald' was quite at home all the time
we had been in South America. He was a good Catholic,

and much caressed by the Spaniards. He attended mass regularly, bowed to all processions, and was in their eyes everything a good Catholic ought to be. He often thought of remaining at Buenos Aires, under the protection of the worthy priest; he had actually agreed to do so when the order for our release arrived. We were to join General Whitelocke on the next day, after fourteen days' confinement. Donald was still wavering, yet most inclined to stay. I sung to him, 'Lochaber no more!'*— the tears started into his eyes—he dashed them off. 'Na, na! I canna stay, I'd maybe *return to Lochaber nae mair.*' The good priest was hurt at his retracting his promise, yet was not offended. He said, 'It is natural. I once loved Spain above all the other parts of the world; but——' Here he checked himself, gave us his blessing and ten doubloons apiece and left us. We immediately upon our release set out on our return to Britain, and had an agreeable and quick passage in which nothing in particular occurred.

NOTES

[1] Sir Samuel Auchmuty (1756–1822), commander of the reinforcements, had decided it was impossible to retake Buenos Aires with the small force at his disposal and so attacked Montevideo instead. He became Commander-in-Chief at Madras in 1810 and Commander-in-Chief in Ireland in 1821.

[2] Lieutenant-General John Whitelocke (1757–1833) had been appointed to command in South America on 24 February, 1807 on the recommendation of the Duke of York. On

Lochaber No More, a popular Scottish song, was written by Allan Ramsay in the 1720s.

his arrival he superseded Sir Samuel Auchmuty. His in-incompetent direction of the attack upon the Spanish in Buenos Aires and his subsequent withdrawal from Monte-video led to his being brought before a court-martial at Chelsea the following year. After a trial lasting seven weeks he was found guilty on a variety of charges and sentenced to be cashiered. This sentence was read out to every regiment in the service, and Whitelocke spent the remaining twenty-five years of his life in retirement.

[3] Major-General John Leveson-Gower was Whitelocke's second-in-command.

[4] Robert Craufurd (1764–1812), known as 'Black Bob', established his reputation as a brilliant commander of light troops in this inglorious campaign in South America. A man of ferocious temper, he was rumoured in the Army to have ordered his men to shoot the bungling Whitelocke if they caught sight of him during the battle.

[5] Colonel William Carr Beresford (1768–1854) escaped after six months' imprisonment and reached England in 1807. He later became one of Wellington's most trusted generals. He was created Lord Beresford of Albuera and Cappoquin after the Peninsular War during which he commanded the Portuguese Army.

[6] The Chevalier de Liniers was a French emigré who had taken command of the Spanish troops.

[7] Donald M'Donald seems to have been the author's only close friend in the Regiment. They had sailed from Leith together. 'He was my bed-fellow and became my firm friend,' the author wrote of their time in the Isle of Wight. 'Often he would get himself into altercations on my behalf. Donald could read and write: this was the sum of his education. He was innocent and ignorant of the world; only eighteen years of age, and had never been a night from home, before he left his father's house. He

had come from Inverness to Edinburgh on foot, with no other intention than to enlist in the 71st. His father had been a soldier in it, and was now living at home after being discharged. Donald called it *his* regiment.'

2

Portugal

1808

After an absence of seventeen months the author sailed for home towards the end of 1807 and landed at the Cove of Cork on Christmas Day. He marched to Middleton Barracks where he wrote to his father, sending the ten doubloons he had received from the priest, and received in reply a letter from his brother to tell him that their father was dead. 'On receipt of this letter, I became unfit to do or think on any thing but the fatal effects of my folly,' he wrote. 'I fell into a lowness of spirits that continued with me until . . . the fatigue and hardship I was forced to undergo on being sent abroad again roused me from my lethargy. I was now more determined to remain with the army, to punish myself, than ever. This I wrote to my brother, and desired him to make my mother as comfortable as possible with the money I had sent.'

At the end of January he left Middleton Barracks for Cork where he remained until 17th June, 1808, when he was 'embarked on an expedition under Sir Arthur Wellesley, consisting of nine regiments of infantry'. Spanish patriots had risen in arms against the French invaders of their country and had asked England for help. The British government had responded by ordering

Wellesley to make a diversionary attack on the French forces in Portugal.

The 71st remained at anchor until 12th July when they set sail for the Portuguese coast. The regiment was brigaded with three battalions of the 60th Rifles, under the command of Brigadier-General Henry Fane. It had a strength of 52 sergeants, 22 drummers and 874 rank and file.

WE BEGAN to disembark [at Mondego Bay] on the 1st of August. The weather was so rough and stormy that we were not all landed until the 7th.[1] On our leaving the ships, each man got four pound of biscuit and four pound of salt beef cooked on board. We marched for twelve miles, up to the knees in sand, which caused us to suffer much from thirst, for the marching made it rise and cover us. We lost four men of our regiment, who died of thirst. We buried them where they fell. At night we came to our camp ground, in a wood, where we found plenty of water, to us more acceptable than any thing besides on earth. We here built large huts and remained four days. We again commenced our march along the coast towards Lisbon. In our advance we found all the villages deserted, except by the old and destitute, who cared not what became of them.

On the 13th there was a small skirmish between the French and our cavalry, after which the French retired. On the 14th we reached a village called Alcobaca which the French had left the night before. Here were a great many wine stores that had been broken open by the French. In a large wine cask we found a French soldier, drowned, with all his accoutrements.

On the morning of the 17th, we were under arms an hour before day. Half an hour after sunrise, we observed the enemy in a wood. We received orders to retreat. Having fallen back about two miles, we struck to the right in order to come upon their flank, whilst the 9th, 29th and 5th battalion of the 60th attacked them in front. They had a very strong position on a hill. The 29th advanced up the hill, not perceiving an ambush of the enemy, which they had placed on each side of the road. As soon as the 29th was right between them they gave a volley which killed or wounded every man in the grenadier company except seven. Unmindful of their loss they drove on and carried the entrenchments. The engagement lasted until about four o'clock when the enemy gave way. We continued the pursuit till darkness put a stop to it. The 71st had only one man killed and one wounded. We were manœuvring all day to turn their flank, so that our fatigue was excessive, though our loss was but small. This was the battle of Roliça, a small town at the entrance of a hilly part of the country.

We marched the whole of the 18th and 19th without meeting any resistance. On the 19th we encamped at the village of Vimiero and took up a position alongst a range of mountains.

On the 20th we marched out of our position to cover the disembarkation of four regiments, under General Anstruther.[2] We saw a few French cavalry who kept manœuvring but did not offer to attack us.

On the 21st we were all under arms an hour before daybreak. After remaining some time, we were dismissed, with orders to parade again at ten o'clock to attend divine service, for this was a Sabbath morning. How unlike the Sabbaths I was wont to enjoy! Had it not been for the situation in which I had placed myself, I could have enjoyed it much.

Vimiero is situated in a lovely valley, through which the small River Maceira winds, adding beauty to one of the sweetest scenes, surrounded on all sides by mountains and the sea, from which the village is distant about three miles. There is a deep ravine that parts the heights, over which the Lourinhã road passes. We were posted on these mountains and had a complete view of the valley below. I here, for a time, indulged in one of the most pleasing reveries I had enjoyed since I left home. I was seated upon the side of a mountain, admiring the beauties beneath. I thought of home—Arthur's Seat and the level between it and the sea all stole over my imagination. I became lost in contemplation and was happy for a time.

Soon my daydream broke and vanished from my sight. The bustle around was great. There was no trace of a day of rest. Many were washing their linen in the river, others cleaning their firelocks; every man was engaged in some employment. In the midst of our preparation for divine service, the French columns began to make their appearance on the opposite hills. 'To arms, to arms!' was beat, at half past eight o'clock. Every thing was packed up as soon as possible, and left on the camp ground.

We marched out two miles to meet the enemy, formed line and lay under cover of a hill for about an hour, until they came to us. We gave them one volley and three cheers—three distinct cheers. Then all was as still as death. They came upon us, crying and shouting, to the very point of our bayonets. Our awful silence and determined advance they could not stand. They put about

B

and fled without much resistance. At this charge we took thirteen guns and one General.[3]

We advanced into a hollow and formed again; then returned in file, from the right in companies, to the rear. The French came down upon us again. We gave them another specimen of a charge, as effectual as our first, and pursued them three miles.

In our first charge I felt my mind waver; a breathless sensation came over me. The silence was appalling. I looked alongst the line. It was enough to assure me. The steady, determined scowl of my companions assured my heart and gave me determination. How unlike the noisy advance of the French! It was in this second charge our piper, George Clark, was wounded in the groin.[4] We remained at our advance until sunset, then retired to our camp ground. The ground was so unequal that I saw little of this battle, which forced the French to evacuate Portugal.

On my return from the pursuit at Montevideo the birds of prey were devouring the slain. Here I beheld a sight, for the first time, even more horrible—the peasantry prowling about, more ferocious than the beasts and birds of prey, finishing the work of death, and carrying away whatever they thought worthy of their grasp. Avarice and revenge were the causes of these horrors. No fallen Frenchman that showed the least signs of life was spared. They even seemed pleased with mangling the dead bodies. When light failed them, they kindled a great fire and remained around it all night, shouting like as many savages. My sickened fancy felt the same as if it were witnessing a feast of cannibals.

Next morning we perceived a column of the enemy upon the sandhills. We were all in arms to receive them, but it turned out to be a flag of truce. We returned to our old camp ground, where we remained three days, during the time the terms of capitulation were arranging. We then got orders to march to Lisbon. On our arrival there, the French flag was flying on all the batteries and forts. We were encamped outside of the town and marched in our guards, next day, to take possession, and relieve all the French guards. At the same time, the French flag was hauled down and we hoisted, in its stead, the Portuguese standard.

We remained in camp until the day the French were to embark. We were then marched in to protect them from the inhabitants; but, notwithstanding all we could do, it was not in our power to hinder some of their sick from being murdered. The Portuguese were so much enraged at our interference in behalf of the French that it was unsafe for two or three soldiers to be seen alone. The French had given the Portuguese much cause to hate them; and the latter are not a people who can quickly forgive an injury, or let slip any means of revenge, however base.

On the 27th October we quitted Lisbon and marched to Abrantes, where we remained fourteen days. Then we marched to Camponia, and remained there, for an order to enter Spain.

NOTES

[1] On landing the 71st were sent from Fane's brigade to that of Brigadier-General Ronald Craufurd Ferguson (1773–1841) whose command also included the 36th and 40th.

[2] Brigadier-General Robert Anstruther (1768–1809). His

brigade consisted of the 20th and 52nd Regiments and four companies of the 95th. He died of exhaustion two days after leading them into Corunna.

[3] This was General Antoine-Françoise Brenier (1767–1832). He was captured by Corporal Mackay of the 71st who was awarded an ensign's commission.

[4] Piper George Clark, though badly wounded, announced 'Deil ha' my saul, if ye shall want music!' and continued playing.

3

Spain
1808-1809

*After his victory at Vimiero, Wellesley had urged his
superior officer, Sir Harry Burrard, to pursue the French
to Lisbon. 'Sir Harry, now is your time to advance,' he
had said to him. 'The enemy are completely beaten and
we shall be in Lisbon in three days.' But Sir Harry did not
agree; nor did Sir Hew Dalrymple who arrived the next
day from Gibraltar to take command. The result was the
humiliating Convention of Cintra which provided that
the French should be transported home in British ships
taking with them all their stores and all that they had
acquired in Portugal.*

*The next month, however, Sir John Moore received a
letter from Downing Street: 'His Majesty, having determined to employ . . . not less than 30,000 infantry and
5,000 cavalry in the North of Spain, to cooperate with
the Spanish armies in the expulsion of the French from
that Kingdom, has been graciously pleased to entrust to
you the Command-in-Chief of this force.'*

*The advance, under Moore, began in October, 1808,
and the 71st crossed the frontier in November.*

THE FIRST place we arrived at in Spain was Badajoz,
where we were very kindly treated by the inhabitants

and Spanish soldiers. We remained there about a fortnight, when the division commanded by General Sir John
Hope,[1] to which I belonged, received orders to march towards Madrid. We halted at El Escorial, about seven
leagues from Madrid, and remained there five days; but
were at length forced to retreat to Salamanca.

Two days before our arrival at Salamanca, we were
forced to form ourselves into a square, to repel the
attacks of the enemy; and in that position we remained
all night. It was one of the severest nights of cold I ever
endured in my life. At that time we wore long hair,
formed into a club at the back of our heads. Mine was
frozen to the ground in the morning and when I
attempted to rise my limbs refused to support me for
some time. I felt the most excruciating pains over all my
body, before the blood began to circulate.

We marched forty-seven miles this day,[2] before encamping, and about nine miles to a town next morning,
where the inhabitants were very kind to us. They brought
out, into the market-place, large tubfuls of accadent* (a
liquor much used in Spain,) that we might take our
pleasure of it; and everything they had that we stood in
need of. This day we were under the necessity of burying
six guns on account of the horses failing, being quite
worn down by fatigue. The headquarters of the army
were at Salamanca. Our division was quartered three
leagues from it, at Alba de Tormes.

On the 14th of December we advanced to a place
called Toro. The roads were bad, the weather very
severe; all around was covered with snow.

---

*Aguadiente, the name by which Spanish brandy was then usually
known.

Our fatigue was dreadful and our sufferings almost more than we could endure.

On the 24th of December our headquarters were at Sahagun. Every heart beat with joy. We were all under arms and formed to attack the enemy. Every mouth breathed hope: 'We will beat them to pieces and have our ease and enjoy ourselves,' said my comrades. I even preferred any short struggle, however severe, to the dreadful way of life we were, at this time, pursuing. With heavy hearts, we received orders to retire to our quarters: 'And won't we be allowed to fight? Sure we'd beat them,' said an Irish lad near me. 'By Saint Patrick, we'd beat them so easy, the General means to march us to death, and fight them after!'

Next morning we fell back upon Mayorga, on the road to Benavente.

On the 25th, Christmas day, we commenced our rout for the sea-coast, melancholy and dejected, sinking under extreme cold and fatigue, as if the very elements had conspired against us. Then commenced the first day of our retreat.

On the 26th it rained the whole day, without intermission. The soil here is of deep rich loam and the roads were knee-deep with clay. To form a regular march was impossible, yet we kept in regiments; but our sufferings were so great that many of our troops lost all their natural activity and spirits, and became savage in their dispositions. The idea of running away from an enemy we had beat with so much ease at Vimiero, without even firing a shot, was too galling to their feelings. Each spoke to his fellow, even in common conversation, with bitterness, rage flashing from their eyes, even on the most trifling occasions of disagreement.

The poor Spaniards had little to expect from such men as these, who blamed them for their inactivity. Everyone found at home was looked upon as a traitor to his country. 'The British are here to fight for the liberty of Spain, and why is not every Spaniard under arms and fighting? The cause is not ours; and are we to be the only sufferers?' Such was the common language of the soldiers; and from these feelings pillage and outrage naturally arose. The conduct of the men, in this respect, called forth, on the 27th, a severe reprimand from the Commander-in-Chief.

We halted at Benavente for one night. Just as the last division of our army entered into the town the drums beat to arms. Every man was on the alert and at his post in an instant. The cavalry poured out at the gates to meet the enemy; but the French did not like the manner and spirit that appeared amongst us. They retired from the heights and we endeavoured to pass the night in the best manner in our power.

28th, the Spaniards now gave us no assistance, save what was enforced. The Duchess of Ossuna has here a castle surpassing any thing I had ever seen. It was such, on our arrival, as I have read the description of, in books of fairy tales. I blush for our men; I would blame them too. Alas, how can I, when I think upon their dreadful situation, fatigued and wet, shivering, perishing with cold? No fuel to be got, not even straw to lie upon. Can men in such a situation admire the beauties of art? Alas! only so far as they relieve his cruel and destroying wants. Everything that would burn was converted into fuel, and even the fires were placed against the walls that they might last longer and burn better. Many of our men slept all night wrapt in rich tapestry which had been torn down to make bed clothes.

Scarce was our rearguard within the town ere the alarm was sounded. We rushed to our posts, pushing the inhabitants out of our way. Women and children crowded the streets, wringing their hands and calling upon their saints for protection. The opposite plain was covered with fugitives. The French, as usual, liked not the spirit with which we formed and the ardour with which our cavalry issued from the gates. They were content to look upon us from the neighbouring heights. The bridges were ordered to be destroyed, which was done before day. That over the Esla had been destroyed to little purpose, as a ford was found only 300 yards farther down the river. The picquets hastened thither and were skirmishing with four squadrons of the Imperial Guards, who had already formed on the bank. The 10th Hussars were sent for. On their arrival, General Stewart,[3] with them and the picquets, charged and drove the Imperial Guard into the river. They crossed in the utmost confusion, but formed on the opposite bank. Some pieces of artillery that had been placed at the bridge soon dispersed them. General Lefebvre,[4] commander of the Imperial Guards, and seventy prisoners, were the fruits of this action. We were told by the Spaniards that Buonaparte saw this affair from the heights.

On the 30th we reached Astorga, which we were led to believe was to be our resting-place, and the end of our fatigues. Here we found the army of General Romana.[5] I can convey no description of it in words. It had more the appearance of a large body of peasants, driven from their homes, famished and in want of everything, than a regular army. Sickness was making dreadful havoc amongst them. It was whispered we were to make a stand here. This was what we all wished, though none believed. We had been told so at Benavente, but our movements had not the smallest appearance of a retreat, in which we were to face about and make a stand; they were more like a shameful flight.

From Astorga to Villafranca del Bierz is about sixty miles. From Salamanca to Astorga may be called the first and easiest part of this tragedy, in which we endured many privations and much fatigue; from Astorga to Villafranca, the second and by far the more severe part. Here we suffered misery without a glimpse of comfort. At Astorga there were a great many pairs of shoes destroyed. Though a fourth of the army were in want of them, and I among the rest, yet they were consumed alongst with the other stores in the magazines.

The first sixteen miles the road lay wholly up the mountain, and the country was open. At this time it was a barren waste of snow. At the top of the mountain is a pass, which is one of the strongest, they say, in Europe. It is about eight or nine miles long. All the way through this pass the silence was only interrupted by the groans of the men, who, unable to proceed farther, laid themselves down in despair to perish in the snow, or where the report of a pistol told the death of a horse, which had fallen down, unable to proceed. I felt an unusual listlessness steal over me. Many times have I said, 'These men who have resigned themselves to their fate are happier than I. What have I to struggle for? Welcome death! happy deliverer!' These thoughts passed in my mind involuntarily. Often have I been awakened out of this state of torpor by my constant friend Donald, when falling out of the line of march to lie down in despair. The rain poured in torrents; the melted snow was half knee-deep in many places, and stained by the blood that flowed from our wounded and bruised feet. To add to our misery, we were forced by turns to drag the baggage. This was more than human nature could sustain. Many wagons were abandoned and much ammunition destroyed. Our arrival at Villafranca closed the second act of our tragedy.

From Villafranca we set out on the 2nd January, 1809. What a New Year's Day had we passed! Drenched with rain, famished with cold and hunger, ignorant when our misery was to cease. This was the most dreadful period of my life. How differently did we pass our *hogmanay* from the manner our friends were passing theirs at home. Not a voice said, 'I wish you a Happy New Year.' Each seemed to look upon his neighbour as an abridgement to his own comforts. His looks seemed to say, 'One or other of the articles you wear would be of great use to me; your shoes are better than those I possess; if you were dead, they would be mine.'

Before we set out there were more magazines destroyed. Great numbers would not leave the town, but concealed themselves in the wine cellars, which they had broken open, and were left there; others after we were gone, followed us. Many came up to the army dreadfully cut and wounded by the French cavalry, who rode through the long lines of these lame defenceless wretches, slashing among them as a schoolboy does amongst thistles. Some of them, faint and bleeding, were forced to pass alongst the line as a warning to others. Cruel warning! Could the urgency of the occasion justify it? There was something in the appearance of these poor, emaciated, lacerated wretches that sickened me to look upon. Many around me said, 'Our commanders are worse than the French. Will they not even let us die in peace, if they cannot help us?' Surely this was one way to brutalize the men and render them familiar to scenes of cruelty.

Dreadful as our former march had been, it was from Villafranca that the march of death may be said to have begun. On the day after we left that place, we were attacked by the French, but drove them back and renewed our forlorn march.

From Villafranca to Castro is one continued toil up Monte del Cebrero. It was one of the sweetest scenes I ever beheld, could our eyes have enjoyed anything that did not minister to our wants. There was nothing to sustain our famished bodies or shelter them from the rain or snow. We were either drenched with rain or crackling with ice. Fuel we could find none. The sick and wounded that we had been still enabled to drag with us in the wagons were now left to perish in the snow. The road was one line of bloody foot-marks from the sore feet of the men; and on its sides lay the dead and the dying. Human nature could do no more. Donald M'Donald, the hardy Highlander, began to fail. He, as well as myself, had long been barefooted and lame;[6] he, that had encouraged me to proceed, now himself lay down to die. For two days he had been almost blind, and unable, from a severe cold, to hold up his head. We sat down together; not a word escaped our lips. We looked around, then at each other, and closed our eyes. We felt there was no hope. We would have given in charge a farewell to our friends; but who was to carry it? There were, not far from us, here and there, above thirty in the same situation with ourselves. There was nothing but groans, mingled with execrations, to be heard, between the pauses of the wind. I attempted to pray and recommend myself to God; but my mind was so confused I could not arrange my ideas. I almost think I was deranged. We had not sat half an hour, sleep was stealing upon me, when I perceived a bustle around me. It was an advanced party of the French. Unconscious of the action, I started upon my feet, levelled my musket, which I had still retained, fired, and formed with the other stragglers. The French faced about and left us. There were more of them than of us. The action, and the approach of danger in a shape which we had it in our power to repel, roused our dormant feelings, and we joined at Castro.

From Castro to Lugo is about forty-eight miles, where we were promised two days' rest. Why should I continue longer this melancholy narrative? Donald fell out again from sickness, and I from lameness and fatigue. When the French arrived, we formed with the others as before, and they fell back. I heard them, more than once, say, as they turned from the points of our bayonets, that they would rather face a hundred fresh Germans than ten dying English, so great was the alarm we caused in them. How mortifying to think, at these moments, that we were suffering all our misery, flying from an enemy who dared not fight us, and fled from us, poor wretches as we were! How unaccountable was our situation! None could be more galling to our feelings. While we ran, they pursued: the moment we faced about, they halted. If we advanced, they retired. Never had we fought but with success; never were we attacked, but we forced them to retire. 'Let us all unite, whether our officers will or not, and annihilate these French cowards, and shew our country it is not our fault that we run thus; let us secure our country from disgrace, and take a sweet revenge.' This was the language of the more spirited men, and in it the others joined, from a hope of relieving their miseries.

With feelings such as these, with a gradual increase of sufferings, we struggled onwards. Towards the close of this journey, my mind became unfit for any minute observation. I only marked what I myself was forced to encounter. How I was sustained, I am unable to conceive. My life was misery. Hunger, cold, and fatigue had deprived death of all its horrors. My present sufferings I felt; what death was, I could only guess. 'I will endure everything, in the hope of living to smooth the closing years of my mother's life, and atone for my unkindness. Merciful God! support me.' These ejaculations were always the close of my melancholy musing; after which I felt a new invigoration, though, many times, my reflections were broken short by scenes of horror that came in my way. One, in particular, I found, after I came home, had been much talked of.

After we had gained the summit of Monte del Castro and were descending, I was roused by a crowd of soldiers. My curiosity prompted me to go to it; I knew it must be no common occurrence that could attract *their* sympathy. Judge of the feelings which I want words to express. In the centre lay a woman, young and lovely, though cold in death, and a child, apparently about six or seven months old, attempting to draw support from the breast of its dead mother. Tears filled every eye, but no one had the power to aid. While we stood around, gazing on the interesting object, then on each other, none offered to speak, each heart was so full. At length one of General Moore's staff-officers came up and desired

the infant to be given to him. He rolled it in his cloak,
amidst the blessings of every spectator. Never shall I
efface the benevolence of his look from my heart, when
he said, 'Unfortunate infant, you will be my future care.'

From the few remaining wagons we had been able
to bring with us, women and children, who had hitherto
sustained, without perishing, all our aggravated sufferings,
were, every now and then, laid out upon the snow,
frozen to death. An old tattered blanket, or some other
piece of garment, was all the burial that was given them.
The soldiers who perished lay uncovered, until the next
fall of snow, or heavy drift, concealed their bodies.

Amidst scenes like these, we arrived at Lugo. Here
we were to have obtained two days' rest; but fate was
not yet weary of enjoying our miseries. On our arrival,
I tried all in my power to find a place for Donald. The
best I could find was a bakehouse. He lay down in one
of the baking troughs. I put a sack over him. In two
minutes, the steam began to rise out of the trough, in
a continued cloud; he fell asleep, and I went in search
of some refreshment. I was not half an hour away,
when I returned with a little bread; he was still asleep,
and as dry as a bone: I was wet as mire. I felt inclined
more than once to wake him. I did not, but lay down
on a sack and fell asleep. I awoke before him, quite dry.
There were three or four more, lying down on the floor
beside me, asleep. My haversack had been rifled while
I slept, and my little store of bread was gone. It was
vain to complain; I had no resource. Cautiously I ex-
amined those around me asleep, but found nothing. Again
I sallied forth and, to my great joy, I saw a soldier lying
unable to rise, he was so drunk. His haversack seemed
pretty full. I went to him and found in it a large piece

of beef and some bread. I scrupled not to appropriate them to myself. I hastened back to Donald and we had a good meal together. I felt stronger and Donald was in better spirits.

The bridges between Villafranca and Lugo had been imperfectly destroyed. The French made their appearance on the 5th of January and took up a position opposite to our rearguard, a small valley only dividing them from it. This night we remained standing in the fields until day broke, our arms piled. The sky was one continued expanse of stars; not a cloud to be seen, and the frost was most intense. Words fail me to express what we suffered from the most dreadful cold. We alternately went to the calm side of each other, to be sheltered from the wind. In this manner, when day at length broke upon us, we had retrograded over two fields from the spot where we had piled our arms. Many had lain down, through the night, overcome by sleep, from which the last trumpet only will awaken them.

On the 6th the enemy attacked our outposts, but were received by our fatigued and famished soldiers with as much bravery as if they had passed the night in comfortable barracks. They repulsed the French in every assault. The sound of the battle roused our drooping hearts. 'Revenge or death!' said my comrades, a savage joy glistening in their eyes. But the day closed without any attack farther on either side.

On the 7th they came upon us again, and were more quickly repulsed than on the day before. From the first moment of the attack, and as long as the French were before us, discipline was restored, and the officers were as punctually obeyed as if we had been on parade at home. We felt not our sufferings, so anxious were we to end them by a victory, which we were certain of obtaining. But Soult[7] seemed to know our spirits better than our own commanders; and, after these two last samples, kept a respectful distance. We stood to our arms until the evening, the enemy in front, amidst snow, rain and storms. Fires were then lighted and we commenced our retreat after dark.

Before our reserve left Lugo, general orders were issued, warning and exhorting us to keep order, and march together; but, alas! how could men observe order amidst such sufferings? or men whose feet were naked and sore keep up with men who, being more fortunate, had better shoes and stronger constitutions? The officers, in many points, suffered as much as the men. I have seen officers of the Guards, and others, worth thousands, with pieces of old blankets wrapt round their feet and legs; the men pointing at them, with a malicious satisfaction, saying, 'There goes three thousand a year;' or, 'There goes the prodigal son, on his return to his father, cured of his wanderings.' Even in the midst of all our sorrows, there was a bitterness of spirit, a savageness of wit, that made a jest of its own miseries.

The great fault of our soldiers, at this time, was an inordinate desire for spirits of any kind. They sacrificed their life and safety for drink, in many ways; for they lay down intoxicated upon the snow and slept the sleep of death; or, staggering behind, were overtaken and cut down by the merciless French soldiers. The most favourable event was to be taken prisoner. So great was their propensity to drown their misery in liquor that we were often exposed to cold and rain for a whole night in order that we might be kept from the wine stores of a neighbouring town.

Why should I detain the reader longer on our march, every day of which was like the day that was past, save in our inability to contend with our hardships?

We arrived at Corunna on the 11th of January, 1809. How shall I describe my sensations at the first sight of the ocean? I felt all my former despondency drop from my mind. My galled feet trod lighter on the icy road. Every face near me seemed to brighten up. Britain and the Sea are two words which cannot be disunited. The sea and home appeared one and the same. We were not cast down at there being no transports or ships of war there. They had been ordered to Vigo, but they were hourly expected.

On the 13th the French made their appearance on the opposite side of the River Mero. They took up a position near a village, called Perillo, on the left flank, and occupied the houses along the river. We could perceive their numbers hourly increasing.

On the 14th they commenced a cannonade on our position; but our artillery soon forced them to withdraw their guns and fall back. On this day our friends the tars, made their appearance and all was bustle, preparing for embarkation. The whole artillery was embarked, save seven six-pounders and one howitzer, which were placed in line, and four Spanish guns, which were kept as a reserve. Our position was such that we could not use many guns. The sick and dismounted cavalry were sent on board with all expedition. I supported my friend Donald, who was now very weak and almost blind.

On my return to the camp I witnessed a most moving scene. The beach was covered with dead horses, and resounded with the reports of the pistols that were carrying this havoc amongst them. The animals, as if

warned by the dead bodies of their fellows, appeared frantic, neighed and screamed in the most frightful manner.
Many broke loose and galloped alongst the beach with their
manes erect and their mouths wide open.

Our preparations continued until the 16th, when
every thing was completed; and we were to begin our
embarkation at four o'clock. About midday we were all
under arms when intelligence arrived that the French
were advancing. We soon perceived them pouring down
upon our right wing; our advanced picquets had commenced firing. The right had a bad position; yet, if we
lost it our ruin was inevitable. Lord William Bentinck's
brigade,[8] composed of the 4th, 42nd, and 50th, had the
honour of sustaining it, against every effort of the French,
although the latter had every advantage in numbers and
artillery. They commenced a heavy fire, from eleven
great guns placed in a most favourable manner on the
hill. Two strong columns advanced on the right wing,
the one along the road, the other skirting its edges. A
third advanced on the centre. A fourth approached slowly
on the left, while a fifth remained half way down the
hill in the same direction, to take advantage of the first
favourable moment. It was at this time that Sir David
Baird[9] had his arm shattered. The space between the two
lines was much intercepted by stone walls and hedges.
It was perceived by Sir John Moore, as the two lines
closed, that the French extended a considerable way be-
yond the right flank of the British; and a strong body of
them were seen advancing up the valley, to turn it. One
half of the fourth was ordered to fall back and form an
obtuse angle with the other half. This was done as
correctly as could be wished, and a severe flanking fire
commenced upon the advancing French. The 50th, after

climbing over an enclosure, got right in front of the French, charged and drove them out of the village of Elvina. In this charge they lost Major Napier,[10] who was wounded and made prisoner. Major Stanhope was mortally wounded.[11] Sir John was at the head of every charge. Every thing was done under his own eye. 'Remember Egypt!' said he; and the 42nd drove all before them, as the gallant 50th had done. The Guards were ordered to their support.[12] Their ammunition being all spent, through some mistake, they were falling back. 'Ammunition is coming, you have your bayonets,' said Sir John. This was enough; onwards they rushed, overturning everything. The enemy kept up their hottest fire upon the spot where they were. It was at this moment Sir John received his death wound. He was borne off the field by six soldiers of the 42nd and the Guards. We now advanced to the support of the right, led by Lord Paget.[13] Colonel Beckwith,[14] with the Rifle Corps, pushed all before him and nearly took one of their cannon; but a very superior column forced him to retire. Lord Paget, however, repulsed this column, and dispersed every thing before him: when, the left wing of the French being quite exposed, they withdrew and attacked our centre, under Manningham[15] and Leith;[16] but, this position being good, they were easily repulsed. They likewise failed in every attempt on our left. A body of them had got possession of a village on the road to Betanzos [Piedralonga], and continued to fire, under cover of it, till dislodged by Lieutenant-Colonel Nicholls.[17] Shortly after this, night put a period to the battle of Corunna.

At ten o'clock General Hope ordered the army to march off the field by brigades, leaving strong picquets to guard the embarkation. I remained in the rearguard, commanded by Major-General Beresford, occupying the lines in front of Corunna. We had made great fires, and a few of the freshest of our men were left to keep them up, and run round them to deceive the enemy.

At dawn there was little to embark save the rearguard and the reserve commanded by Major-General Hill,[18] who had occupied a promontory behind Corunna. We were scarcely arrived on the beach ere the French began to fire upon the transports in the harbour from the heights of Santa Lucia. Then all became a scene of confusion. Several of the masters of the transports cut their cables. Four of the transports ran ashore. Not having time to get them off, we were forced to burn them. The ships of war soon silenced the French guns and we saw no more of them. There was no regularity in our taking the boats. The transport that I got to had part of seven regiments on board.

The Spaniards are a courageous people; the women waved their handkerchiefs to us from the rocks, whilst the men manned the batteries against the French, to cover our embarkation. Unmindful of themselves, they braved a superior enemy to assist a friend who was unable to afford them further relief, whom they had no prospect of ever seeing again.

Secure within the wooden walls, bad as our condition was, I felt comparatively happy in being so fortunate as to be on board the same vessel with Donald. In relieving his wants, I felt less my own, and was less teased by the wit and ribaldry of my fellow-sufferers who, now that they were regularly served with provisions, and exempt from the fatigues of marching and the miseries of cold, were as happy, in their rags and full bellies, as any men in England.

For two days after we came on board I felt the most severe pains through my whole body; the change was so great, from the extreme cold of the winter nights, which we had passed almost without covering, to the suffocating heat of a crowded transport. This was not the most disagreeable part: vermin began to abound. We had not been without them in our march; but now we had dozens for [each] one we had then. In vain we killed them; they appeared to increase from the ragged and dirty clothes, of which we had no means of freeing ourselves. Complaint was vain. Many were worse than myself; I had escaped without a wound, and, thank God! though I had not a shirt upon my back, I had my health, after the first two days, as well as I ever had it.

On the morning of the tenth day after our embarkation, I was condoling with Donald, who was now quite blind. 'I will never be a soldier again, O Thomas! I will be nothing but Donald the blind man. Had I been killed, if you had left me to die in Spain, it would have been far better to have lain still in a wreath of snow than be, all my life, a blind beggar, a burden on my friends. Oh! if it would please God to take my life from me!'

'Land ahead! Old England once again!' was called from mouth to mouth. Donald burst into tears. 'I shall never see Scotland again; it is me that is the poor dark man!' A hundred ideas rushed upon my mind, and overcame me. Donald clasped me to his breast; our tears flowed uninterrupted.

We anchored that same day at Plymouth, but were not allowed to land; our Colonel kept us on board until we got new clothing. Upon our landing, the people came round us, showing all manner of kindness, carrying the lame and leading the blind. We were received into every house as if we had been their own relations. How proud did I feel to belong to such a people!

NOTES

[1] Lieutenant-General the Hon. John Hope (1765–1823). In 1816 he succeeded his half-brother as Earl of Hopetoun. The three brigades in his division were commanded by James Leith, Rowland Hill and Catlin Crawfurd. The author's battalion was in Crawfurd's brigade together with the 1st Battalion, 36th Regiment and the 1st Battalion, 92nd Regiment.

[2] The forty-seven miles to Peñaranda was actually covered in thirty-six hours. But a day's march of over forty miles was not uncommon.

[8] Brigadier-General Charles William Stewart (1778-1854). He became third Marquess of Londonderry on his brother's death in 1822. His brigade, consisting of the 10th Hussars, 18th Light Dragoons and 3rd Light Dragoons, King's German Legion, were covering the advance of Hope's division.

[4] General Comte Charles Lefebvre-Desnouëttes (1773–1822). Hearing that Napoleon himself had watched the action, he commented gloomily that the Emperor never forgave the unfortunate. However, he was appointed to command the Guard light cavalry at Waterloo.

[5] Pedro Caro y Sureda, The Marqués de la Romana (1761–1811). A hero to the Spanish people, he had been unwillingly performing garrison duties for Napoleon in North Germany when the arrival of a British fleet enabled him to dash aboard with his troops whom he had brought back to drive the French from his homeland. Henry

Crabb Robinson, *The Times* correspondent, described him as looking 'like a Spanish barber'.

[6] The regiment's shoes had been worn out before the retreat began, but they had never been replaced.

[7] Nicolas-Jean de Dieu Soult, Duke of Dalmatia (1769–1851), commander of the French army in the Peninsula.

[8] Major-General Lord William Bentinck (1774–1839), second son of the Duke of Portland, later became Governor-General of India.

[9] Lieutenant-General Sir David Baird (1757–1829). His division had landed at Corunna in October. He had advanced to meet Moore but had been ordered to wait at Astorga, and then, on 7th December, to retreat on Corunna.

[10] Major Charles Napier (1782–1853) brother of George, the future general, and of William, whose history of the Peninsular War was to become one of the great epic narratives of war. He was a great-great-grandson of Charles II and Louise de Kéroualle. He was in command of the 50th as the colonel had obtained leave of absence. Although five times wounded at Corunna, he survived to achieve lasting fame as General Sir Charles Napier, conqueror of Scinde.

[11] Major the Hon. Charles Stanhope (1785–1809), half-brother of Lady Hester Stanhope, was one of Napier's company commanders.

[12] The 1st and 2nd Battalions, the First Foot Guards were in Major-General Henry Warde's brigade in Baird's division.

[13] Henry William Paget, later Earl of Uxbridge and Marquess of Anglesey (1768–1854), was commander of the Cavalry Division.

[14] Lieutenant-Colonel Thomas Sydney Beckwith (1772–1831),

commanding officer of the 95th. A fine commander of light troops, he was knighted in 1815 and promoted Lieutenant-General in 1830.

15 Colonel Coote Manningham. His brigade, which was in Baird's division, comprised the 1st, 26th and 81st Regiments. He died as a consequence of his sufferings in the campaign.

16 Major-General James Leith (1763–1816). His brigade, in Hope's division, comprised the 51st and 76th Regiments and the 2nd Battalion, the 59th.

17 Commanding officer of the 14th Regiment.

18 Major-General Rowland Hill (1772–1842). He served with distinction throughout the Peninsular War after which he was raised to the peerage. He commanded a corps at Waterloo; and was appointed to the command of the Army in 1828 on Wellington's becoming Prime Minister.

4

The Walcheren Expedition
1809

From Plymouth the 71st marched to barracks at Ashford in Kent where they remained for five weeks before moving to camp at Gosport 'where the army was forming a secret expedition'. This was the expedition to Walcheren, an island at the mouth of the Scheldt, on whose southern tip stands the port of Flushing. The object of the expedition, in the words of the orders given to the Commander-in-Chief, Lieutenant-General the Earl of Chatham, the eldest son of the statesman, were 'the capture or destruction of the enemy's ships either building at Antwerp and Flushing or afloat in the Scheldt, the destruction of the Arsenals and dockyards at Antwerp, Terneuse and Flushing, the reduction of the island of Walcheren and the rendering, if possible, the Scheldt no longer navigable for ships of war'.

WE SAILED from the Downs on the 28th July [1809] and reached Flushing in thirty hours, where we landed without opposition. Our regiment was the first that disembarked. We were brigaded, alongside with the 68th and 85th regiments, under the command of Major-General

[Baron] De Rottenburg. Here again, as in South America, I was forced to work in the trenches, in forming the batteries against Flushing.

On the night of the 7th of August the French sallied out upon our works, but were quickly forced back with great loss. They were so drunk, many of them, that they could not defend themselves; neither could they run away: we, in fact, gave up the pursuit, our hearts would not allow us to kill such helpless wretches, a number of whom could not even ask for mercy.

On the evening of the 10th we had a dreadful storm of thunder and rain. At the same time the French Governor opened the sluices and broke down the sea dikes, when the water poured in upon us and we were forced to leave the trenches. However, on the 13th, in the evening, we commenced a dreadful fire upon the town, from the batteries and vessels in the harbour, which threw bombs and rockets on one side, whilst the batteries plyed them with round-shot on the other. I was stunned and bewildered by the noise, the bursting of bombs and falling of chimneys, all adding to the incessant roar of the artillery. The smoke of the burning houses and guns formed, altogether, a scene not to be remembered but with horror, which was increased, at every cessation from firing, (which was very short) by the piercing shrieks of the inhabitants, the wailings of distress and howling of dogs. The impression was such as can never be effaced. After night fell, the firing ceased, save from the mortar batteries. The noise was not so dreadful. The eye was now the sense that conveyed horror to the mind. The enemy had set fire to Old Flushing, whilst the New Town was kept burning by the shells and rockets. The dark flare of the burning, the reflection on the water and sky, made all the space, as far as the eye could reach, appear an abyss of fire. The faint tracks of the bombs and luminous train of the rockets, darting towards and falling into the flames, conveyed an idea to my mind so appalling that I turned away and shuddered.

This night our regiment was advanced a good way in front, upon a sea dike, through which the enemy had made a cut, to let the water in upon our works. Towards midnight, when the tide was ebb, Colonel Pack[1] made a sally into one of the enemy's batteries. We crossed the cut in silence; Colonel Pack entered first and struck off the sentinel's head at one blow. We spiked their guns, after a severe brush. At the commencement, as I leaped into the works, an officer seized my firelock before I could recover my balance, and was in the act to cut me down; the sword was descending, when the push of a bayonet forced him to the ground. It was Donald, who fell upon us both. I extricated myself as soon as possible, rose and fell to work. There was no time to congratulate. The enemy had commenced a heavy fire upon us, and we were forced to retire with forty prisoners. We lost a great number of men, killed, wounded, and missing. Donald was amongst the latter, but joined in the morning.

Next morning Monnet[2] surrendered and we marched into Flushing, scarce a house of which had escaped; all was a scene of death and desolation.

The wet and fatigue of the last few days had made me ill. I was scarce able to stand, yet I did not report myself sick. I thought it would wear off. Next night I was upon guard. The night was clear and chill; a thin white vapour seemed to extend around as far as I could see; the only part free from it were the sand heights. It covered the low place where we lay and was such as you see early in the morning, before the sun is risen, but more dense. I felt very uncomfortable in it; my two hours, I thought, never would expire; I could not breathe with freedom. Next morning I was in a burning fever at times, at other times trembling and chilled with cold. I was unfit to rise or walk upon my feet. The surgeon told me I had taken the country disorder. I was sent to the hospital; my disease was the same as that of which hundreds were dying. My spirits never left me; a ray of hope would break in upon me, the moment I got ease, between the attacks of this most severe malady.[8]

I was sent, with many others, to Bradburn Lees, where I remained eight weeks ill—very ill indeed. All the time I was in the hospital, my soul was oppressed by the distresses of my fellow-sufferers, and shocked at the conduct of the hospital men. Often have I seen them fighting over the expiring bodies of the patients, their eyes not yet closed in death, for articles of apparel that two had seized at once; cursing and oaths mingling with the dying groans and prayers of the poor sufferers. How dreadful to think, as they were carried from each side of me, it might be my turn next! There was none to comfort, none to give a drink of water, with a pleasant countenance. I had now time to reflect with bitterness on my past conduct; here I learned the value of a parent's kindness.

I had been unable to write since my illness, and I longed to tell my mother where I was, that I might hear from her. I crawled along the wall of the hospital to the door, to see if I could find one more convalescent than myself, to bring me paper. I could not trust the hospital men with the money. To see the face of heaven and

breathe the pure air was a great inducement to this diffi-
cult exertion. I feebly, and with anxious joy, pushed
open the door! Horrid moment, dreadful sight! Donald
lay upon the barrow, at the stair-head, to be carried to
the dead-room; his face was uncovered, and part of his
body naked. The light forsook my eyes, I became dreadfully sick and fell upon the body. When I recovered
again, there was a vacancy of thought and incoherence
of ideas that remained with me for some time; and it
was long before I could open a door without feeling an
unpleasant sensation.

When I became convalescent I soon recovered my
wonted health. The regiment arrived at Bradburn Lees
upon Christmas day, and I commenced my duties as a
soldier. By the death of Donald I had again become a
solitary individual; nor did I again form a friendship,
while we lay here, which was until May, 1810, at which
time, we got the rout for Deal. We remained there until
the month of September, when an order came for a
draught of 600 men for service in Portugal, of which
number I was one.

NOTES

¹ Lieutenant-Colonel Denis Pack (1772–1823), the Irish commanding officer of the author's Regiment. A son of Dr
Thomas Pack, Dean of Kilkenny, he had been gazetted
cornet in the 14th Light Dragoons in 1791 and had
commanded the 71st since 1800. After being wounded
three times and taken prisoner in South America, he took
the Regiment to Portugal in 1808 and was in command
throughout the retreat to Corunna. Having distinguished
himself during the Walcheren expedition, he was
appointed to a Portuguese brigade under Beresford. Pro-

moted to Major-General in 1813, he was knighted in 1815 and commanded a brigade of Picton's division at Water-loo where he was wounded for the twelfth time. He was a well-liked and respected commanding officer of the 71st. During the retreat to Corunna—when many officers inexperienced in foraging for themselves were driven to asking their men for scraps of food—Colonel Pack sent a request for the heart of a bullock which his men had acquired. They sent him not only the heart but the kidneys as well.

[2] Louis-Claude, Baron Monnet (1766–1819).

[3] The fever, which took such a heavy toll, was caused by the enemy's opening of the sluices. This not only flooded the trenches, as Thomas records, but sent up a noisome, dense miasma from the overflowing Walcheren ditches. Fever was accompanied by dysentery and typhus which swept through the ranks taking a fearful toll. In one battalion every single soldier was affected; and of those who recovered many were afterwards unfit for further service. The 71st escaped more lightly than other regi-ments which was attributed to their taking a medicine of brandy and gunpowder recommended by the Navy.

5

From Lisbon to Fuentes de Oñoro
1810–1811

After Soult's repulse at Corunna, the French forces in the Peninsula had been reorganized and Marshal Massena, in command of the Army of Portugal, had received orders to clear the country of British troops. Wellesley, now Lord Wellington, had built the defensive lines of Torres Vedras behind which he withdrew in safety after his defeat of Massena at Busaco on 27th September, 1810. A fortnight before the battle, the author embarked at Deal for Lisbon. Colonel Pack having been promoted, Lieutenant-Colonel Sir Nathaniel Levett Peacock assumed temporary command of the 71st which, owing to its continued sickness, could muster only six companies.

THERE were six companies of 100 men each, embarked in two frigates, 300 in each. I was on board the *Melpomene*.

During the six days' sail to Lisbon, my thoughts were not the most agreeable. I was on my way to that country in which I had already suffered so much. My health was good but my spirits were very low. I could not yet bring myself to associate with the other men, so

as to feel pleasure in their amusements. I found it necessary to humour them in many things and be obliging to
all. I was still called saucy* and courted by my comrades
to join them. I had changed my bedfellow more than
once; they not liking my dry manner, as they called it.

On the seventh day after leaving Deal we were
landed at Blackhorse Square, Lisbon,[1] amidst the shouts
of the inhabitants. We were marched to the top of the
town and billeted in a convent. A good many were
billeted in the town, the convent being not large enough
to contain us. I was billeted upon a cook-shop.

Two years before, while encamped before Lisbon, I
had often wished to enter the town; now I as ardently
wished to leave it. I was sickened every hour of the day
with the smell of garlic and oil. Everything there is fried
in oil that will fry. Oil and garlic is their universal relish.
Cleanliness they have not the least conception of. The
town is a dunghill from end to end; their principal squares
are not even free from heaps of filth. You may make a
shift to walk by the side of streets with clean shoes; but
cross one, if you dare. I inquired at one of our regiment,
who had been left sick, if they had any scavengers?
'Yes,' said he, 'they have one.' 'He will have a great
many under him?' 'None.' 'What folly, to have only
one to such a city!' 'And that one, only when he may
please to come.' 'You joke with me.' 'No, I don't. The
rain is their street-cleaner; he will be here soon; there
will be clean streets while he remains; then they prepare
work for him again.'

To my great joy we paraded in the grand square
on the seventh day after our arrival and marched, in

*Saucy then meant didactic and opinionated rather than cheeky.

C

sections, to the music of our bugles, to join the army, having got our camp equipments, consisting of a camp-kettle and bill-hook to every six men, a blanket, a canteen and haversack to each man. Orders had been given that each soldier, on his march, should carry alongst with him three days' provision. Our mess of six cast lots who should be cook the first day, as we were to carry the kettle day about. The lot fell to me. My knapsack contained two shirts, two pairs of stockings, one pair overalls, two shoe-brushes, a shaving-box, one pair spare shoes, and a few other articles; my greatcoat and blanket above the knapsack; my canteen with water was slung over my shoulder on one side, my haversack with beef and bread on the other; sixty round of ball cartridge, and the camp-kettle above all.

I was now well broke down, by what I had been in my first campaign with Moore. How different was Tom, marching to school, with his satchel on his back, from Tom, with his musket and kit, a private soldier, an atom of an army, unheeded by all, his comforts sacrificed to ambition, his untimely death talked of with indifference, and only counted in the gross with hundreds, without a sigh.

We halted, on the first night, at a palace belonging to the Queen of Portugal, called Mafra, where we were joined by the Honourable Henry Cadogan, our Colonel.[2] Next day, the 14th of October, 1810, we joined the army at Sobral de Monte Agraça, a small town surrounded by hills. On the front is a hill, called by our men 'Windmill Hill', from a number of windmills which were upon it; in the rear, another they called 'Gallows Hill', from a gibbet standing there.

We had not been three hours in the town, and were

busy cooking, when the alarm sounded. There were nine British and three Portuguese regiments in the town. We were all drawn up and remained under arms, expecting every moment to receive the enemy, whose skirmishers covered Windmill Hill. In about an hour the light companies of all the regiments were ordered out, alongst with the 71st. Colonel Cadogan called to us, at the foot of the hill, 'My lads, this is the first affair I have ever been in with you; show me what you can do, now or never.' We gave a hurra and advanced up the hill, driving their advanced skirmishers before us, until about half way up, when we commenced a heavy fire and were as hotly received. In the meantime, the remaining regiments evacuated the town. The enemy pressed so hard upon us we were forced to make the best of our way down the hill and were closely followed by the French, through the town, up Gallows Hill. We got behind a mud wall and kept our ground in spite of their utmost efforts. Here we lay upon our arms all night.

Next morning, by daybreak, there was not a Frenchman to be seen. As soon as the sun was fairly up we advanced into the town and began a search for provisions, which were now become very scarce; and to our great joy found a large store-house full of dry fish, flour, rice and sugar, besides bales of cloth. All now became bustle and mirth; fires were kindled and every man became a cook. Scones were the order of the day. Neither flour nor sugar were wanting and the water was plenty; so I fell to make myself a flour scone. Mine was mixed and laid upon the fire, and I, hungry enough, watching it. Though neither neat nor comely, I was anticipating the moment when it would be eatable. Scarce was it warm ere the bugle sounded to arms. Then was the joy that reigned a moment before turned to execrations. I snatched my scone off the fire, raw as it was, put it into my haversack and formed. We remained under arms until dark and then took up our old quarters upon Gallows Hill, where I ate my raw scone, sweetly seasoned by hunger. In our advance to the town, we were much entertained by some of our men who had got over a wall the day before, when the enemy were in the rear, and now were put to their shifts to get over again and scarce could make it out.

Next morning the French advanced to a mud wall about forty yards in front of the one we lay behind. It rained heavily this day and there was very little firing. During the night we received orders to cover the bugle and tartans of our bonnets with black crape, which had been served out to us during the day, and to put on our great coats. Next morning the French, seeing us thus, thought we had retired and left Portuguese to guard the heights. With dreadful shouts, they leaped over that wall before which they had stood, when guarded by the British. We were scarce able to withstand their fury. To retreat was impossible; all behind being ploughed land, rendered deep by the rain. There was not a moment to hesitate. To it we fell, pell-mell, French and British mixed together. It was a trial of strength in single combat; every man had his opponent, many had two. I got one up to the wall, on the point of my bayonet. He was unhurt. I would have spared him, but he would not spare himself. He cursed and defied me, nor ceased to attack my life, until he fell, pierced by my bayonet. His breath died away, in a curse and menace. This was the work of a moment; I was compelled to this extremity. I was again attacked, but my antagonist fell, pierced by a random shot. We soon forced them to retire over the wall, cursing their mistake. At this moment I stood gasping for breath, not a shoe on my feet; my bonnet had fallen to the ground. Unmindful of my situation, I followed the enemy over the wall. We pursued them about a mile and then fell back to the scene of our struggle. It was covered with dead and wounded, bonnets and shoes trampled and stuck in the mud. I recovered a pair of shoes; whether they had been mine or not I cannot tell; they were good.

Here I first got any plunder. A French soldier lay upon the ground dead; he had fallen backwards; his hat had fallen off his head, which was kept up by his knapsack. I struck the hat with my foot, and felt it rattle; seized it in a moment and, in the lining, found a gold watch and silver crucifix. I kept them; as I had as good a right to them as any other. Yet they were not valuable in my estimation. At this time, life was held by so uncertain a tenure, and my comforts were so scanty, that I would have given the watch for a good meal and a dry shirt. There was not a dry stitch on my back at the time, nor for the next two days.

In a short time the French sent in a flag of truce for leave to carry off their wounded, which was granted. They advanced to their old ground and we lay looking at each other for three days, the two first of which the rain never ceased to pour; the third day was good and dry. During this time, the French withdrew their lines and left only picquets.

On the third day an officer and twelve men went to the wall, as the French sentinels were become very remiss. He looked over and saw a picquet of fifty men, playing cards and amusing themselves. Our party levelled their muskets, and gave them a volley. They took to their heels, officers and all. There was no further attack made that day and we retired behind the line of batteries at night, quite worn out with hunger and fatigue.

For five nights I had never been in bed and, during a good part of that time, it had rained hard. We were upon ploughed land, which was rendered so soft that we sunk over the shoes at every step. The manner in which I passed the night was thus: I placed my canteen upon the ground, put my knapsack above, and sat upon it, supporting my head upon my hands; my musket between my knees, resting upon my shoulder, and my blanket over all, ready to start in a moment, at the least alarm. The nights were chill; indeed, in the morning I was so stiff I could not stand or move with ease for some time; my legs were benumbed to the knees. I was completely wet three nights out of the five. A great number of the men took the fever and ague after we retired behind the lines. I was not a whit the worse.

On our arrival behind the lines, our brigade, consisting of the 50th, 71st, and 92nd, commanded by Major-General Sir William Erskine,[3] was quartered in a small village called Sabreira. Our first care was to place outposts and sentinels between the batteries, about twenty yards distant from each other. We communicated with the Foot Guards on our right and the Brunswick infantry on our left. Those off duty were employed throwing up batteries and breast-works, or breaking up the roads. The day after we fell into the lines, the French placed sentinels in front of us, without any dispute. There was a small valley and stream of water between us.

We remained thus for five weeks; every day, when off duty, forming defensive works, or breaking up the roads; it being a place that no army could pass, save upon the highway. The advanced picquet of the French lay in a windmill; ours, consisting of one captain, two subalterns and 400 men, in a small village. There was only a distance of about 150 yards between us. We learned, from the deserters, that the French were much in want of provisions. To provoke them our sentinels, at times, would fix a biscuit to the point of their bayonets and present to them. One day the French had a bullock, in endeavouring to kill which the butcher missed his blow and the animal ran off right into our lines. The French looked so foolish. We hurraed at them, secured the bullock, brought him in front, killed him in style. They looked on, but dared not approach to seize him. Shortly after, an officer and four men came with a flag of truce and supplicated in the most humble manner for the half of the bullock, which they got for godsake.

On the evening of the 14th November the French made their outposts stronger than they had yet been, and kindled great fires after dark. We were all under arms an hour before day, expecting to be attacked; but when the day dawned there was not a Frenchman to be seen. As soon as the sun was up, we set off after them.

When we arrived at Sobral, we found a great number of our men, who had been wounded on the 14th and 15th October, besides a greater proportion of French wounded and sick. We were told by our men that the weakly men and the baggage of the French army had been sent off eight days before. We were halted at Sobral until provisions came up, when three days allowance was served out to each man. We again commenced our advance. The weather was very bad; it rained for a great part of the time without intermission. On the fourth day we took about 100 prisoners, who had concealed themselves in a wood.

This retreat brought to my mind the Corunna race. We could not advance 100 yards without seeing dead soldiers of the enemy, stretched upon the road or at a little distance from it, who had laid down to die, unable to proceed through hunger and fatigue. We could not pity them, miserable as they were. Their retreat resembled more that of famished wolves than men. Murder and devastation marked their way; every house was a sepulchre, a cabin of horrors! Our soldiers, used to wonder why the Frenchmen were not swept by heaven from the earth, when they witnessed their cruelties. In a small town called Mafra I saw twelve dead bodies lying in one house upon the floor! Every house contained traces of their wanton barbarity. Often has a shade of doubt crossed my mind, when reading the accounts of former atrocities; often would I think—they are exaggerated—thank God we live in more civilized times. How dreadfully were my doubts removed. I cease to describe, lest I raise doubts similar to my own.

At this time I got a distaste I could never overcome. A few of us went into a wine-store where there was a large tun with a ladder to get to the top, in which was a hole about two feet square. There was not much wine in it, so we buckled our canteen straps together, until a camp-kettle attached to them reached the liquor. We drew it up once—we all drank; down it went again—it got entangled with something at the bottom of the tun—a candle was lowered; to our great disappoinment, the corpse of a French soldier lay upon the bottom! Sickness came upon me and, for a long time afterwards, I shuddered at the sight of red wine. The Portuguese

soldiers never would drink red wine if white wine could
be got. When I asked the reason, their reply was they
knew how it was made.

We continued our pursuit, every day taking more
or less prisoners, who were unable to keep up with the
main army, until we came in front of Santarem. Here
we piled arms upon the sandy ground; the French were
in possession of the heights. Colonel Cadogan made the
smartest of the men run races, in front, for rum. From
this sport we were suddenly called to form line for
attack; but the French position was too strong for us.
By this time it was quite dark and we had a large plain
to cross to a village where we were to halt all night. In
our march we were put into confusion and a good number of the men knocked over by a flock of goats, of
which we caught a few, which made a delicious supper
for us. On our arrival at the village we were forced to
break up the doors, as the inhabitants would not let us in.

Next morning was very wet. The following evening,
we halted at a village; but two Portuguese regiments
had been before us and swept all away. We sent out
parties to forage, and got some Indian corn, which we
ground ourselves at a mill, the inhabitants having all
fled. We were then quartered in a convent in Alcanterina,
where we lay from the beginning of December until
5th March, 1811. Provisions were very scarce. Fatigue
parties were sent out every day for Indian corn and pot
herbs. We had beef; but we could not subsist upon beef
alone, which was seldom good, being far driven, very
tough, and lean. An accident procured us a short relief:
some of our men, amusing themselves in piercing the
ceiling with their bayonets, discovered a trap-door, and
found a great concealed store of food and valuables.

We fared well while it lasted. Having very little duty, our time was spent at football. We were very badly off for shoes, but, by good luck, discovered a quantity of leather in a tan-yard. Those who found it helped themselves first, and were wasting it. The Colonel then ordered each man a pair of soles and heels, to be put up in his knapsack.

The French gave us the slip at the commencement of their retreat by placing wooden guns in their batteries, and stuffing old clothes with straw, which they put in place of their sentinels. By this means their retreat was not discovered for two days, and only then by one of our cavalry riding up to their lines to take a sentinel prisoner, who appeared asleep. As soon as it was ascertained there was a trick, we set off after them, and, beginning to come up with them, took a good many prisoners. Our advance was so rapid that provisions could not be brought up to us. We were often two days without bread. The rear of the army being always served first, we, who were in advance, seldom got enough. For four or five days we were so close up with the French that we had skirmishes with them every day; but, having received no bread for three days, we were forced to halt for two, until we got a supply. During these two days I had an opportunity of witnessing the desolation caused by the French soldiers. In one small village I counted seventeen dead bodies of men, women, and children; and most of the houses were burnt to the ground.

The Portuguese were not unrevenged of their destroyers, great numbers of whom had lain down, unable to proceed, from wounds or fatigue, and had been either killed by the peasantry, or died, unheard, amongst the devastation themselves or their fellows had made.

At this time we were forced either to forage or starve, as we were far in advance of our supplies. I was now as much a soldier as any of my comrades, when it fell to my turn. At this time I was so fortunate as to procure the full of my haversack of Indian corn heads, which we used to call turkeys. I was welcomed with joy; we rubbed out some of our corn and boiled it with a piece of beef, roasted some of our turkeys and were happy. Bread at length coming up, we received three days allowance a man, and recommenced our advance; but never came up with the enemy, until they reached the Agueda, on the 9th April, 1811.

We were marched into winter quarters. Our division, the 2nd, was posted in a small town called Albergaria, on the frontiers of Spain, where we remained till the 30th April. During our stay, I had an adventure of a disagreeable kind. I was strolling as usual when I heard a voice pleading in the most earnest manner, in great distress. I hastened to the spot and found a Portuguese muleteer taking a bundle from a girl. I ran up to him and bade him desist. He flew into a passion, drew his knife and made a stab at me. I knocked him down with my fist; the girl screamed and wept. I stood on my guard, and bade him throw away his knife. He rose, his eyes glistening with rage, and stabbed furiously at me. In vain I called to him. I drew my bayonet. I had no choice; yet, unwilling to kill, I held it by the point and knocked him to the ground with the hilt, as he rushed to close with me, left him there and brought home the weeping girl to her parents.

On the 30th April we set off for Fuentes de Oñoro, where we arrived, after a fatiguing march of three days; and formed line, about two miles in rear of the town, hungry and weary, having had no bread for the last two days.

On the 3rd of May, at daybreak, all the cavalry and sixteen light companies occupied the town. We stood under arms until three o'clock, when a staff-officer rode up to our Colonel and gave orders for our advance. Colonel Cadogan put himself at our head, saying, 'My lads, you have had no provision these two days; there is plenty in the hollow in front, let us down and divide it.' We advanced as quick as we could run and met the light companies retreating as fast as they could. We continued to advance, at double quick time, our firelocks at the trail, our bonnets in our hands. They called to us, 'Seventy-first, you will come back quicker than you advance.' We soon came full in front of the enemy. The Colonel cries, 'Here is food, my lads, cut away.' Thrice we waved our bonnets, and thrice we cheered; brought our firelocks to the charge, and forced them back through the town.

How different the duty of the French officers from ours. They, stimulating the men by their example, the men vociferating, each chaffing each until they appear in a fury, shouting, to the points of our bayonets. After the first huzza the British officers, restraining their men, still as death. 'Steady, lads, steady,' is all you hear, and that in an undertone.

The French had lost a great number of men in the streets. We pursued them about a mile out of the town, trampling over the dead and wounded; but their cavalry bore down upon us and forced us back into the town, where we kept our ground, in spite of their utmost efforts.

In this affair my life was most wonderfully preserved. In forcing the French through the town, during our first advance, a bayonet went through between my side and clothes, to my knapsack, which stopped its progress. The Frenchman to whom the bayonet belonged fell, pierced by a musket ball from my rear-rank man. Whilst freeing myself from the bayonet, a ball took off part of my right shoulder wing and killed my rear-rank man, who fell upon me. Narrow as this escape was, I felt no uneasiness; I was become so inured to danger and fatigue.

During this day the loss of men was great. In our retreat back to the town, when we halted to check the enemy, who bore hard upon us in their attempts to break our line, often was I obliged to stand with a foot upon each side of a wounded man, who wrung my soul with prayers I could not answer, and pierced my heart with his cries to be lifted out of the way of the cavalry. While my heart bled for them, I have shaken them rudely off.

We kept up our fire until long after dark. About one o'clock in the morning, we got four ounces of bread served out to each man, which had been collected out of the haversacks of the Foot Guards. After the firing had ceased we began to search through the town, and found plenty of flour, bacon and sausages, on which we feasted heartily, and lay down in our blankets, wearied to death. My shoulder was as black as a coal, from the recoil of my musket; for this day I had fired 107 round of ball-cartridge. Sore as I was, I slept as sound as a top till I was awakened by the loud call of the bugle an hour before day.

Soon as it was light the firing commenced and was kept up until about ten o'clock, when Lieutenant Stewart, of our regiment, was sent with a flag of truce for leave to carry off our wounded from the enemy's lines, which was granted; and, at the same time, they carried off theirs from ours. As soon as the wounded were all got in, many of whom had lain bleeding all night, many both a day and a night, the French brought down a number of bands of music to a level piece of ground, about ninety or a hundred yards broad, that lay between us. They continued to play until sunset, whilst the men were dancing and diverting themselves at football. We were busy cooking the remainder of our sausages, bacon and flour.

After dark a deserter from the French told us that there were five regiments of grenadiers picked out to storm the town. In the French army, the grenadiers are all in regiments by themselves. We lay down, fully accoutred as usual, and slept in our blankets. An hour before day we were ready to receive the enemy.

About half-past nine o'clock a great gun from the French line, which was answered by one from ours, was the signal to engage. Down they came, shouting as usual. We kept them at bay, in spite of their cries and formidable looks. How different their appearance from ours! Their hats, set round with feathers, their beards long and black, gave them a fierce look. Their stature was superior to ours; most of us were young. We looked like boys; they like savages. But we had the true spirit in us. We foiled them in every attempt to take the town until about eleven o'clock when we were overpowered and forced through the streets, contesting every inch.

A French dragoon, who was dealing death around, forced his way up to near where I stood. Every moment I expected to be cut down. My piece was empty; there was not a moment to lose. I got a stab at him, beneath the ribs, upwards; he gave a back stroke, before he fell, and cut the stock of my musket in two. Thus I stood unarmed. I soon got another and fell to work again.

During the preceding night we had been reinforced by the 79th regiment, Colonel Cameron commanding, who was killed about this time.[4] Notwithstanding all our efforts, the enemy forced us out of the town, then halted and formed close column betwixt us and it. While they stood thus, the havoc amongst them was dreadful. Gap after gap was made by our cannon, and as quickly filled up. Our loss was not so severe, as we stood in open files. While we stood thus, firing at each other as quick as we could, the 88th regiment advanced from the lines, charged the enemy and forced them to give way. As we passed over the ground where they had stood, it lay two and three deep of dead and wounded. While we drove them before us through the town, in turn they were reinforced, which only served to increase the slaughter. We forced them out and kept possession all day.

After sunset the enemy sent in a flag of truce, for leave to carry off their wounded and bury their dead, which was granted. About ten o'clock we were relieved and retired back to our lines. In these affairs we lost four officers and two taken prisoners, besides 400 men killed and wounded. This statement, more than any words of mine, will give an idea of the action at Fuentes de Oñoro.[5]

NOTES

[1] The name commonly given by the British to the Praça do Commercio because of the bronze equestrian statue of Joseph I which was erected in its centre in 1775.

² The Hon. Henry Cadogan (1780–1813), son of the 3rd Baron Cadogan and 1st Earl (second creation, 1800). Having purchased an ensignship in the 18th (Royal Irish) Regiment, he afterwards bought a company in the 60th, exchanged to the Coldstream Guards, then became lieutenant-colonel in his old regiment before exchanging to the 71st Highlanders in 1808. He assumed command of the 71st in succession to Lieutenant-Colonel Sir Nathaniel Peacock. A greatly respected commanding officer he was celebrated for his ability to encourage his men in battle with colourful and inspiring words of command. He was killed at Vitoria. His last words were 'God bless my brave countrymen'.

³ Major-General Sir William Erskine (1769–1813), a brave not to say foolhardy officer whose increasingly obvious symptoms of insanity led to his being required to leave the Army. He killed himself by jumping out of a high window in Lisbon.

⁴ Lieutenant-Colonel Philip Cameron, elder son of Major-General Sir Alan Cameron. 'I hope you will derive some consolation,' Wellington wrote to the father, 'that he fell in the performance of his duty at the head of your brave regiment, loved and respected by all that knew him.'

⁵ After the battle of Fuentes de Oñoro, of which Wellington said, 'If Boney had been there we should have been damnably licked', the 71st were reduced to less than 200 men.

6

From Badajoz to Bejar
1811-1813

Their heavy losses had left the 71st with less than two hundred men fit for duty. The author himself had been lucky to escape. After the fighting at Fuentes de Oñoro, he found that a musket ball had pierced the centre of his knapsack and dented the back of his shoe-brush. When the French retired the remains of the Regiment were sent back to their old quarters at Albergaria to wait for reinforcements.

[While at Albergaria] we received a draught of 350 men, and again set off. Our division consisted of the 24th, 42nd, 50th, 71st, 79th, 92nd, and one battalion of the King's German Legion. We were assembled after dark and marched off all that night, next day, and night following, when we arrived at a town, situated upon a hill, called Pennemacore. The heat was so great we were unable to keep together. I do not believe that ten men of a company marched into the town together; they had lain down upon the road, or straggled behind, unable to climb the hill. Two men belonging to the Foot Guards fell down dead, and one of the 50th, from heat and thirst. Two or three times my sight grew dim; my mouth was dry as dust, my lips one continued blister. I had water in my canteen but it tasted bitter as soot, and it was so warm it made me sick. At this time, I first tried a thing which gave me a little relief; I put a small pebble into my mouth, and sucked it. This I always did afterwards, in similar situations, and found drought easier to be borne.

Early next morning, the 50th, 71st, and 92nd were marched on; and the remainder of the division returned to their old quarters at Albergaria. After a most distressing march of seven days we arrived at Badajoz, where we remained one night; then marched nine miles to a town called Talavera [La] Real, where we halted three days; then marched, at six o'clock in the evening, to the camp at Albuera, a few days after the battle which had been the cause of our rapid movement. We remained in camp at Albuera a short time; then marched to Elvas, a strong town on the Portuguese frontier, opposite Badajoz. We remained here four days; and then marched into camp, at Toro de Moro, where we remained for a considerable time.

Here I enjoyed the beauties of the country more than at any former period. Often, when off duty, have I wandered into the woods to enjoy the cool refreshing shade of the cork trees, and breathe the richly perfumed air, loaded with the fragrance of innumerable aromatic plants. One evening, as I lay in the woods thinking upon home, sweeter than all the surrounding sweets, almost overcome by my sensations, I heard, at a small distance, music. I listened some time ere I could be satisfied it was so. It ceased all at once; then began sweeter then before. I arose, and approached nearer, to avoid the noise of a small burn that ran rippling near where I had been reclining. I soon knew the air. I crept nearer and could distinguish the words. I became rivetted to the spot. That moment compensated for all I had suffered in Spain. I felt that pleasure which softens the heart, and overflows at the eyes. The words that first struck my ear, were,

Why did I leave my Jeanie, my daddy's cot, an' a',
To wander from my country, sweet Caledonia.

Soon as the voice ceased, I looked through the under-wood and saw four or five soldiers seated on the turf, who sung in their turn, Scotland's sweetest songs of remembrance. When they retired, I felt as if I was bereft of all enjoyment. I slowly retired to the camp, to reflect and spend a sleepless night. Every opportunity, I returned to the scene of my happiness and had the pleasure, more than once, to enjoy this company unseen.

While encamped here, we received a draft of 350 men from England. Shortly after, we marched to Borba, to protect the siege of Badajoz. We lay here till the 17th June, when Soult raised the siege, and we retired to Portalegre. We then were marched to Castelo de Vide, another hill town, about two leagues from Portalegre.

On the 22nd October, we received information that General Girard,[1] with 4,000 men, infantry and cavalry, was collecting contributions in Estremadura, and had cut off part of our baggage and supplies. We immediately set off from Portalegre, along with the brigade com-manded by General Hill, and, after a most fatiguing march, the weather very bad, we arrived at Malpartida. The French were only ten miles distant. By a near cut, on the Merida road, through Aldea del Cano, we got close up to them, on the 27th, at Alcuescar, and were drawn up in columns, with great guns, ready to receive them. They had heard nothing of our approach. We went into the town. It was now nigh ten o'clock; the enemy were in Arroyo dos Molinos, only three miles distant. We got half a pound of rice served out to each man, to be cooked immediately. Hunger made little cooking necessary. The officers had orders to keep their men silent. We were placed in the houses; but our wet and heavy accoutrements were on no account to be taken off. At twelve o'clock we received our allowance of rum and, shortly after, the sergeants tapped at the doors, calling not above their breath. We turned out and, at slow time, continued our march.

The whole night was one continued pour of rain. Weary and wet to the skin, we trudged on, without exchanging a word; nothing breaking the silence of the night save the howling of the wolves. The tread of the men was drowned by the pattering of the rain. When day at length broke we were close upon the town. The French posts had been withdrawn into it, but the embers still glowed in their fires. During the whole march the 71st had been with the cavalry and horse-artillery as an advanced guard.

General Hill rode up to our Colonel, and ordered him to make us clean out our pans,[2] (as the rain had wet all the priming) form square and retire a short distance, lest the French cavalry had seen us and should make an attack. However, the drift was so thick they could not; it blew right in their faces when they looked our way. The Colonel told us off in three divisions and gave us orders to charge up three separate streets of the town and force our way, without halting, to the other side. We shouldered our arms. The General, taking off his hat, said, 'God be with you—quick march.' On reaching the gates we gave three cheers, and in we went, the inhabitants calling, 'Live the English', our piper playing 'Hey Johnny Cope',[3] the French swearing, fighting in confusion, running here and there, some in their shirts, some half accoutred. The streets were crowded with baggage and men ready to march, all now in one heap of confusion. On we drove. Our orders were to take no prisoners and neither to turn to the right nor left until we reached the other side of the town.

As we advanced I saw the French General [Girard] come out of a house, frantic with rage. Never will I forget the grotesque figure he made as he threw his cocked hat upon the ground and stamped upon it, gnashing his teeth. When I got the first glance of him he had many medals on his breast. In a minute his coat was as bare as a private's.

We formed, under cover of some old walls. A brigade of French stood in view. We got orders to fire; not ten pieces in a company went off, the powder was again so wet with the rain. A brigade of Portuguese artillery came up. We gave the enemy another volley, leaped the wall, formed column and drove them over the hill, down which they threw all their baggage, before they surrendered. In this affair, we took about 3,000 prisoners, 1,600 horse, and 6 pieces of artillery, with a great quantity of baggage, etc.

We were again marched back to Portalegre where the horses were sold and divided amongst the men, according to their rank. I got 2s. 6d. for my share; but I had provided myself a good assortment of necessaries out of the French stores at Arroyo dos Molinos.

We remained at Portalegre, until the campaign began, in the month of January, 1812. We were in advance, covering the operations against Ciudad Rodrigo and Bada-joz. We had a most fatiguing spring, marching and counter-marching between Merida and Almandralejo. We were first marched to Merida, but Dombrowski[4] fled with the utmost precipitation. We then marched against Drouet,[5] who was at Almandralejo; but he, likewise, set off for Zafra, leaving his stores and ammunition, to us a welcome gift. The weather was so wet the very shoes were soaked off our feet, and many were the contrivances we fell upon to keep them on.

Almandralejo is a low swampy place, the worst town I ever was in in Spain. Our men called it Almandralejo Craco (cursed). Seldom a day passed but we had a skirmish with the enemy at Merida or Almandralejo.

In the month of March we got the route for Albuera, where we formed our lines and were working at the batteries day and night. An alarm was given three different times, and we were marched on to the position, but nothing occurred and we fell back.

When I first came upon the spot where the battle of Albuera had been fought* I felt very sad; the whole ground was still covered with the wrecks of an army, bonnets, cartridge-boxes, pieces of belts, old clothes and shoes; the ground in numerous ridges, under which lay many a heap of mouldering bones. It was a melancholy sight; it made us all very dull for a short time.

The whole army receiving orders to advance, we moved in solid columns, cavalry on right and left. The enemy fell back as we advanced. Our brigade was marched up a hill, where we had a beautiful view of the armies, threatening each other, like two thunder clouds

*On 16 May, the year before.

charged with death. Shortly after we were marched into the valley, the enemy fired two or three round shot at us, which did no harm. We were encamped till next day at noon, when we set off, pursuing them for two days, and were then marched back to Almandralejo Craco, where we lay till the beginning of April.

Next we advanced to cover the operations against Badajoz, which surrendered on the 6th, the day of our arrival. Next morning the band played 'The Downfall of Paris'. We remained until May, when we were marched to Almaraz, where the French had two forts which intercepted our supplies, as they commanded the bridge over the Tagus.

Our brigade consisting of the 50th, 71st, and 92nd regiments, set off and marched all day until noon. On the second day our officers got orders that every person in the village of Almaraz should be put to death, there being none but those belonging to the enemy in it. We marched all night, until break of day next morning, when we halted on a height opposite the large fort, just as they fired their morning gun. As the day broke up, they got sight of our arrival and gave us a shell or two, which did us no harm. We were moved down the hill out of their view. Then we were marched to the height again, where we stood under arms for a short time, until we were ordered to pile arms and take off our packs. We remained thus until twelve o'clock, when we got half an allowance of liquor. Oxen were brought up and killed on the spot; each man received two pounds of beef in lieu of bread. We got this for three days.

On the evening of the third day General Hill ordered our left companies to move down to the valley to cover his recognisance. When he returned the officers were called. A scaling-ladder was given to each section of a company of the left wing, with the exception of two companies. We moved down the hill in a dismal manner; it was so dark we could not see three yards before us. The hill was very steep, and we were forced to wade through whins and scramble down rocks, still carrying the ladders. When daylight on the morning of the 19th at length showed us to each other, we were scattered all over the foot of the hill like strayed sheep, not more in one place than were held together by a ladder. We halted, formed, and collected the ladders, then moved on. We had a hollow to pass through to get at the battery. The French had cut a part of the brae-face away, and had a gun that swept right through into the hollow. We made a rush past it, to get under the brae on the other side. The French were busy cooking and preparing to support the other fort, thinking we would attack it first, as we had lain next it.

On our approach the French sentinel fired and retired. We halted, fixed bayonets and moved on in double quick time. We did not receive above four shots from the battery until we were under the works and had the ladders placed to the walls. Their entrenchment proved deeper than we expected, which caused us to splice our ladders under the wall; during which time, they annoyed us much by throwing grenades, stones and logs over it; but not a Frenchman durst be seen on the top; for we stood with our pieces cocked and presented. As soon as the ladders were spliced, we forced them from the works, and out of the town, at the point of the bayonet, down the hill, and over the bridge. They were in such haste they cut the bridge before all their men had got over, and numbers were either drowned or taken prisoners.

One of our men had the honour to be the first to mount the works.

Fort Napoleon fired two or three shot into Fort Almaraz. We took the hint from this circumstance, and turned the guns of Almaraz on Fort Napoleon, and forced the enemy to leave it. It being a bridge of boats, two companies were sent with brooms to burn and cut it away; but the enemy, being in superior force upon the other side, compelled them to retire under cover, until reinforced.

We moved forward to the village of Almaraz and found plenty of provisions, which had been very scarce with us for some days. We filled our haversacks and burned the town, then encamped close by it all night and marched next morning, leaving a company of sappers and miners to blow up the works. We marched back to our old quarters, and continued marching up and down, watching the motions of the enemy.

On the night of the 22nd July, when we were in a wood, we received the joyful news of the defeat of Marmont[6] at Salamanca, and got a double allowance of liquor. Colonel Cadogan took the end of a horn, called *a tot*, and drank, 'Success to the British arms'. Some of us had money and sent to the village for liquor. We made a little treat, in the best manner we could, and passed a joyful night.

We advanced to Aranjuez, where we lay for some time. It is a palace of the King of Spain. The whole country is beautiful; fruit was very plenty, and of all kinds. We were eight days in the Escurial, and continued to watch the motions of the French alongst the Tagus, skirmishing almost every day. Individuals of the 13th and 14th Light Dragoons used to engage in single combat with the horsemen of the enemy. Often whole squadrons would be brought to engage by two men beginning.

We remained thus skirmishing till Lord Wellington raised the siege of Burgos; when we fell back to the Iacamah on the beginning of November; then on Alba de Tormes where we skirmished two days and two nights. A part of us here were lining a wall, the French in great strength in front. One of our lads let his hat fall over, when taking cartridges from it, laid his musket against the wall, went over to the enemy's side and came back again unhurt. At this very time, the button of my stock was shot off.

The short time we remained at Alba de Tormes we were very ill off for provisions. One of our men, Thomas Cadwell, found a piece of meat near the hospital, on the face of the brae. He brought it home and cooked it. A good part of it was eaten before one of the men, perceiving him, said, 'What is that you are eating?' Tom said it was meat he had found. The others looked and knew it to be the forearm of a man. The hand was not at it; it was only the part from a little below the elbow and above the wrist. The man threw it away but never looked squeamish; he said it was very sweet and was never a bit worse.

The French left strong picquets in front, stole down the river and crossed, hoping to surprise us and come upon our rear. We immediately blew up the bridge and retired. Many of our men had to ford the river. We left a Spanish garrison in the fort and retired to the heights.

There was a mill on the riverside, near the bridge, wherein a number of our men were helping themselves to flour, during the time the others were fording. Our Colonel rode down and forced them out, throwing a handful of flour on each man as he passed out of the mill. When we were drawn up on the heights, he rode along the column, looking for the millers, as we called them. At this moment a hen put her head out of his coat-pocket, and looked first to one side, and then to another. We began to laugh; we could not restrain ourselves. He looked amazed and furious at us, then around. At length the Major rode up to him, and requested him to kill the fowl outright, and put it into his pocket. The Colonel, in his turn, laughed, called his servant, and the millers were no more looked after.

We moved along the heights for two or three miles, towards the main body of the army; and lay down in column for a few minutes, until Lord Wellington came up and reconnoitred the movements of the enemy, when we immediately got orders to follow the line of march. We continued to follow, for some time, until we came to a place covered over with old ammunition barrels and the wrecks of an army. This was the ground the battle of Salamanca had been fought on. We got not a moment to reflect. The word was given, 'Fix bayonets, throw off all lumber', and we were moved up the hill at double quick time. We pushed up as hard as possible, reached the top almost out of breath and met the enemy right in front. They were not twenty paces from us. We gave them a volley. Two companies of the German Legion were sent to keep them in play whilst the lines were forming. Two brigades came up at double quick time. We formed in three lines and forced them to retire. They lost, in their flight, a great number of men by the fire of our cannon.

After dark we withdrew our lines and encamped in a wood. We were in great want of necessaries, having very little bread or beef amongst us, and no water. I set off in quest of some, slung round with canteens belonging to the mess. After searching about for a long time, faint and weary, I was going to give up in despair and sat down to reflect what I should do. Numbers were moving around, looking anxiously for water of any kind; quality was of no moment. I thought I heard a bustle on my right. I leaped up, ran towards it; I heard voices and the croaking of frogs. Tempting sound! I stopped not to reflect. As I drew near, the sound became more distinct; I heard the welcome words, 'Water, water'. In I ran, up to the knees amongst mules and men, and, putting down my head, drank a sweet draught of it, dirty as it was; then filled my canteens and came off quite happy. The croaking of the frogs was pleasanter music, at that time, and more welcome, than any other sound. When I came to the camp ground, I was welcomed with joy. We got our allowance of liquor, and mixed it with the water; then lay down and slept till an hour before day, when we moved on to our old position on the hills. The French lay in column close by Salamanca. We remained there till Lord Wellington perceived the French were endeavouring to get into our rear to cut off our communications, they being very superior in force. The army received orders to draw up in column and move off in brigades, each brigade in succession, leaving the 71st for the rearguard.

I, at this time, got a post, being for fatigue with other four. We were sent to break biscuit and make a mess for Lord Wellington's hounds. I was very hungry and thought it a good job at the time, as we got our own fill, while we broke the biscuit—a thing I had not got for some days. When thus engaged, the prodigal son never once was out of my mind, and I sighed, as I fed the dogs, over my humble situation and ruined hopes.

As we followed the army Colonel Cadogan made us halt in a plain upon ploughed land where he began to drill us. We were wet and weary and like to faint with hunger. The ground was so soft from the rain we could scarce keep the step. The French were coming down from the heights. 'Now,' says he, 'there they are; if you are not quicker in your movements, I will leave you every one to them.' At this moment, General Hill's aide-de-camp rode up, saying, 'Move on, and cover the brigade of artillery, by the General's order, or you will be all prisoners in five minutes.' We immediately left off drill, and marched on until dark, under a heavy rain and over miserable roads; one shoe in our hand, the other on our knapsack.

As we entered a wood, we were agreeably annoyed by the grunting of hogs and squeaking of pigs. 'There is a town here,' says my comrade. We all longed for 'pile arms'. At length the word was given and cooks ordered to cut wood. More cooks than one turned out of each mess and went in different directions in search of forage. All this time the whole wood resounded with the reports of muskets. It resembled a wood contested by the enemy. At length our cooks returned, one with a pig, another with a skin of wine, or with flour, and we made a hearty supper and lay down happy and contented.

Next morning we continued the line of march under a heavy rain; the horses were scarce able to drag the cannon through the mud. We marched thus about eight miles and halted at a village, where we encamped and cooked the remains of our pork. Everyone was engaged cooking or cutting wood when the French made their appearance on the opposite heights. The bugle sounded to fall in; immediately we formed square to receive cavalry. They galloped down close to our square. We had not time to load our pieces and many of us were only half accoutred, they had come so quick upon us. Many of them were very much in liquor. Three or four galloped into the centre of our square; we opened to receive them. A brigade of guns coming to our relief, they put to the right about and fled. We stood under arms for some time. A brigade of French infantry was drawn up on the opposite heights. It being only their advanced guard, Lord Wellington gave orders to pile arms but to remain accoutred. We stood in this position, the rain pouring upon us, until we were forced to lie down through fatigue.

Day at length appearing, we got orders to move on, after the army in sections, the enemy having retired through the night. We had not moved thus two miles, until the French advance came down upon us, picking up every individual who fell out. The cries of the women and children were dreadful, as we left them.[7] We were retiring in square, playing a howitzer from the centre to keep their cavalry in check. We continued to move on in this manner, sending out the left company to fire and retire. The rain poured; the roads were knee-deep; when one had to stop, all were obliged to stop. Each of the enemy's cavalry had a foot soldier behind him, who formed when they came close. When we were halted, and advanced to charge, they mounted and retired.

At length we forded the Agueda and encamped on the opposite side. Rearguards and quarter-guards were immediately sent out and picquets planted. We were not an hour and a half encamped, when a dreadful firing commenced on our left. We were all under arms in a moment. The firing continued very severe for the space of two hours. We then piled arms and began to cut wood to lay under us, that the water might run below, as the rain continued to pour in torrents. We might as well have lain in the river. We were up, an hour before day, and wrung out our blankets, emptied our shoes of the water, each man trembling like the leaf of a tree. We followed the line of march for about four leagues and encamped in a plain, expecting to be attacked every moment. The French did not advance this night.

Next night we marched into a town. Sergeants were called out for quarters and we were put in by sections, into the best quarters they could find. This town we called the *reeky* town; it was the most smoky place I ever was in. The sergeants got two months' pay for each man; every one had a little. Canteens were immediately in requisition; wine and *accadent* were the only words you could hear. Three dollars* for wine and one for accadent made a joyful night and a merry mess. We had no care; the song went round. We were as merry as if we had not suffered in our retreat. The recollection of our wants made our present enjoyments doubly dear. Next morning we did the best we could to clean ourselves; but we made a very shabby figure. Our haversacks were black with grease; we could not get the marks of the pork out all we could do.

Here we remained eight days, then marched to Porto Banyes, where we received a draught of 150 men from England and stayed about eight days, then marched to Monte Moso. We got here a new kit. Before this we were

*A Spanish dollar was worth about five shillings at this time.

completely in rags, and it used to be our daily labour to pick the vermin off ourselves. We were quartered in the villages until Colonel Cadogan arrived from England, who inspected and reviewed us in our new clothes. We looked very well. The Colonel told us we were 'as fat as fowls'.

During the time the 50th were in Bejar, the French made an attempt to surprise it. We were marched up to it at double quick time. We ran uphill for four miles and were formed in the town and marched up to the walls, making as great a show as possible. The French stood in column on the opposite side of the town. We had picquets of the 50th posted on the outside. Bejar being a town of great trade, the French hoped to get a supply of clothing, but finding they could not succeed, they retired, and we went back to our old cantonments.

In a few days we relieved the 50th and marched into Bejar, at which place we remained all winter and until the month of May, 1813, when the campaign commenced.

I got a most excellent billet. Everything was in plenty, fruit in abundance. I was regarded as a son of the family, partook with them at meals and, if anything was better than another, my part was in it. I amused myself, when off duty, in teaching the children to read, for which my hosts thought they never could be grateful enough.

I have often thought the Spaniards resembled the Scots in their manner of treating their children. How has my heart warmed, when I have seen the father, with his wife by his side, and the children round them, repeating the Lord's prayer and the 23rd Psalm at evening before they went to bed! Once a week the children were

catechised. When I told them they did the same in Scotland they looked at me with astonishment, and asked
'If heretics did so?' The priests often drew comparisons
much to our disadvantage from the conduct of our men.
They even said every heretic in England was as bad as
them.

One afternoon I had walked into the churchyard
and, after having wandered through it, I lay down in the
shade of the wall, near a grave that appeared to have
been lately made. While lying thus, I heard a sob. I
looked towards the place whence it came and perceived
a beautiful female kneeling beside a grave, devoutly
counting her rosary, her tears falling fast upon the
ground. I lay, afraid to move, lest the noise might disturb
her. She remained for some time, absorbed in devotion,
then rose from her knees and, taking a small jar of holy
water, sprinkled the grave and retired undisturbed by
me. I mentioned the circumstance to no one, but, day
after day, I was an unperceived witness of this scene.
At length, she saw me as she approached and was retiring
in haste. I came near her. She stood to let me pass. I said,
'My presence shall give you no uneasiness. Adieu!' 'Stay,'
she said. 'Are you Don Galves' good soldier?' I replied,
'I live with him.' 'Stay, you can feel for me. I have none
to feel for, nor advise me. Blessed Virgin, be my friend!'
She looked to heaven, her eyes beaming resignation and
hope, the tears dropping on her bosom. I stretched out
my hand to her; my eyes, I believe, were wet, I did not
speak. 'None,' she said mournfully, 'can again have my
hand. I gave it to Francisco.' ' 'Tis the hand of friendship.'
'I can have no friend but death. You do not pray for
the dead; you cannot pray with me.' I said, 'I will listen
to yours.' She then began her usual prayers, then rose

D

and sprinkled the grave with holy water. I inquired, 'Whose grave do you water?' 'My mother's.' 'How long has she been dead?' 'Five years.' 'Five years! have you done thus so long?' 'Alas, no! my mother has been released [from purgatory]; but five weeks ago my mournful task again began: 'tis for Francisco. Adieu,' she sobbed, and retired with a hurried step. I dare not embellish, lest this incident should not be credited; but I feel this is a cold account of what passed. I have not taken away, neither have I added a word that did not pass between us. From Galves I learned that Francisco had fallen in a guerrilla party. It is the belief in Spain that every drop of holy water sprinkled upon the grave quenches a flame in purgatory.

We had passed the winter in the most agreeable manner. We lived well; the inhabitants were on good terms with us; we had every thing in abundance and amusements were not wanting. We had bullfights, at which we used to exhibit our powers. Several of our men were hurt. Our horsemen were particularly good bullfighters and the women used to give them great praise. Often we had dancings in the evening; sometimes we got two or three of our band, and then we had dancing in style. Wine and mirth we never wanted. Music was our great want.

The peasants used to dance to the sound of their rattles, consisting of two pieces of hard wood, which they held between their fingers, and by shaking their hands, kept time, in the same manner as the boys in Edinburgh and other parts play what they call 'cockledum ditt'. They call them 'castanetts'.

They have one dance which I never saw in any other place; they call it 'fandango'. I can hardly say it is a dance, for it is scarcely decent. The dancers first run to each other, as if they are looking for one another; then the woman runs away, the man follows; next he runs, and she follows. This they do alternately, all the time using the most expressive gestures, until both seem overcome, when they retire and another couple take their place. This dance had a great effect upon us; but the Spaniards saw it without being moved, and laughed at the quick breathing and amorous looks of our men.

The winter in Bejar was the shortest I ever passed in Spain, yet we remained in that town until May, 1813. The only disagreeable thing was that the wolves, which were very numerous, used to visit us at our advanced posts, when on duty through the night.

One night, while on duty at the bridge, I thought I was to have fallen prey to a very large wolf. My orders were to be on the alert and, if I heard the least sound, to place my ear upon the ground, to distinguish if it were the tread of men or of horses and give the alarm. The night was starry and a little cloudy, when, about half past one o'clock, I could distinguish the tread of an animal. I believed it to be a stray mule or ass, but at length could distinguish a large wolf, a few yards from the bridge, in the middle of the road, looking full upon me. I levelled my piece and stood, my eyes fixed on his. I durst not fire lest I should miss him and give a false alarm. I expected him every moment to spring upon me. We stood thus looking upon each other until the tread of the sergeant and guard to relieve me were heard; then the beast scampered off and relieved me from my disagreeable situation.

NOTES

¹ Jean-Baptiste, Baron Girard (1775–1815).

² The pan was the part of the firelock which contained the priming or powder. When it was wet the flint sparks failed to ignite the charge. In 1807, the Rev. Alexander John Forsyth, the Scottish inventor, obtained a patent for priming with a fulminating powder made of chlorate of potash, sulphur and charcoal, which exploded by percussion. But this invention had not yet been adopted by the Army and was not, indeed, made use of until shortly before Forsyth's death in 1843.

³ *Hey, Johnnie Cope, are ye wauking yet?*
Or are your drums a-beating yet?

This was a ballad written in 1745 by the Scottish song-writer, Adam Skirving (1719–1803), to a tune popular in his day. Sir John Cope was Commander-in-Chief of the forces in Scotland during the rebellion of 1745. At Prestonpans he was caught unawares by the rebels early on the morning of 21st September; and most of his troops were killed or taken prisoner.

⁴ Jan Henryk Dombrowski (1755–1818), a Polish general in Napoleon's service.

⁵ Jean-Baptiste Drouet, Count d'Erlon (1765–1844), commander of the French 9th Corps. He was entrusted by Napoleon with the command of the French right wing at Waterloo.

⁶ Auguste Frédéric Louis Viesse de Marmont, Duke of Ragusa (1774–1852). He had succeeded Massena as commander of the French army. Severely wounded in the battle of Salamanca, he returned to France to recover.

⁷ It was customary at that time to allow a certain proportion of soldiers to bring their wives on foreign service with them. About five women were allowed for each company.

7

Across the Pyrenees
1813-1814

By the beginning of May, Wellington had assembled 52,000 British troops under his command, as well as 29,000 Portuguese, and was ready for the final battles of the long campaign.

MAY CAME at length and we were obliged to leave our kind hosts. I never before felt regret at quitting a town in Spain. That morning we marched, the town was deserted by its inhabitants, who accompanied us a good way; girls weeping and running into the ranks to be protected from their parents, and hanging upon their old acquaintances; parents tearing away and scolding their children; soldiers and inhabitants singing, or exchanging adieus. Almost every man had his handkerchief on the muzzle of his firelock. Don Galves' children, weeping, took leave of me. I never saw them again. May God bless them!

At length we were left to reflect upon our absent friends and commence the toils of war afresh. We lay in camp until the whole army joined, then were reviewed by Lord Wellington and received orders to take the line of march and follow the enemy.

We marched over a great part of Spain, quite across the country, many parts of which were very beautiful, more particularly that before we crossed the Ebro. But we were so harassed by fatigue in our long marches that we never left the camp; and were too weary to pay much attention to any thing that did not relieve our wants.

We continued to advance, until the 20th June, when, reaching the neighbourhood of Vitoria, we encamped upon the face of a hill. Provisions were very scarce. We had not a bit of tobacco and were smoking leaves and herbs. Colonel Cadogan rode away and got us half a pound of tobacco a man, which was most welcome.

Next morning we got up as usual. The first pipes played for parade; the second did not play at the usual time. We began to suspect all was not right. We remained thus until eleven o'clock, then received orders to fall in and follow the line of march. During our march we fell to one side, to allow a brigade of guns to pass us at full speed. 'Now,' said my comrades, 'we will have work to do before night.' We crossed a river and, as we passed through a village, we saw, on the other side of the road, the French camp and their fires still burning just as they had left them. Not a shot had been fired at this time. We observed a large Spanish column moving along the heights on our right. We halted and drew up in column. Orders were given to brush out our locks, oil them and examine our flints. We being in the rear, these were soon followed by orders to open out from the centre, to allow the 71st to advance. Forward we moved up the hill. The firing was now very heavy. Our rear had not engaged before word came for the Doctor to assist Colonel Cadogan who was wounded. Immediately we charged up the hill, the piper playing, 'Hey Johnny Cope'. The French had possession of the top, but we soon forced them back and drew up in column on the height, sending out four companies to our left to skirmish. The remainder moved on to the opposite height. As we advanced, driving them before us, a French officer, a pretty fellow, was pricking and forcing his men to stand. They heeded him not; he was very harsh. 'Down with him!' cried one near me, and down he fell, pierced by more than one ball.

Scarce were we upon the height when a heavy column, dressed in greatcoats, with white covers on their hats, exactly resembling the Spanish, gave us a volley, which put us to the right about at double quick time down the hill, the French close behind, through the whins. The four companies got the word the French were on them. They likewise thought them Spaniards, until they got a volley that killed or wounded almost every one of them. We retired to the height, covered by the 50th, who gave the pursuing column a volley which checked their speed. We moved up the remains of our shattered regiment to the height. Being in great want of ammunition, we were again served with sixty rounds a man, and kept up our fire for some time, until the bugle sounded to cease firing.

We lay on the height for some time. Our drought was excessive; there was no water upon the height, save one small spring, which was rendered useless. One of our men in the heat of the action, called out he would have a drink, let the world go as it would. He stooped to drink; a ball pierced his head; he fell with it in the well, which was discoloured by brains and blood. Thirsty as we were, we could not taste it.

At this time, the Major had the command.[1] There were not 300 of us on the height able to do duty, out of above 1,000 who drew rations in the morning. The cries of the wounded were most heartrending.

The French, on the opposite height, were getting under arms. We could give no assistance, as the enemy appeared to be six to one of us. Our orders were to maintain the height while there was a man of us. The word was given to shoulder arms. The French, at the same moment, got under arms. The engagement began in the plains. The French were amazed, and soon put to the right about through Vitoria. We followed as quick as our weary limbs would carry us. Our legs were full of thorns and our feet bruised upon the roots of the trees. Coming to a bean field at the bottom of the heights, immediately the column was broke and every man filled his haversack. We continued to advance until it was dark and then encamped on a height above Vitoria.

This was the dullest encampment I ever made. We had left 700 men behind. None spoke; each hung his head, mourning the loss of a friend and comrade. About twelve o'clock, a man of each company was sent to receive half a pound of flour for each man, at the rate of our morning's strength, so that there was more than could be used by those who had escaped. I had fired 108 rounds this day. Next morning we awoke dull, stiff and weary. I could scarce touch my head with my right hand; my shoulder was as black as coal. We washed out our firelocks, and moved on again about twelve o'clock, in the line of march.

Towards the afternoon of the 22nd, the day after the battle of Vitoria, a great number of our men joined, who had made their escape, after being taken the day before. We encamped and passed a night of congratulations; mutual hardships made us all brothers. The slain were forgot in our joy for those we had gained thus unexpectedly. Next morning we made a more respectable appearance on parade, being now about 800 strong.[2] The day following we continued our march. In the afternoon we had a dreadful storm of thunder and rain. A Portuguese officer and his horse were killed by it. We encamped upon the face of a hill, the rain continuing to pour. The storm not abating, we could not get our tents up and were exposed all night to its violence.

Next day we arrived before Pamplona, where we lay for some time. One night we were ordered under arms at twelve o'clock. The report was that Pamplona was to be stormed. We marched until daybreak, then drew up in a hollow in the rear of the town, when we got orders to fall back to our old camp ground.

Soon after, we were relieved by a division of Spanish and marched towards the Pyrenees, where we soon fell in with our old playfellows the French, and had a very severe skirmish in the front of the village of Maya. The regiment was divided into two columns, the right commanded by Major [Leslie] Walker, the left by Major [Maxwell] M'Kenzie. We remained under arms all night, the French keeping up their fire. Next morning we forced them over the heights, into their own country, in style; then encamped.

Fatigue parties were called to make rows and rainworks.[3] Our two rear companies were appointed to move to the heights in the rear, upon the first alarm, and maintain them while a man should remain. The signal was three great guns, on the report of the first of which every man was to stand to his arms. One day we sent out a fatigue party to cut wood to make arm-racks. They were not come back when a gun was fired. We stood to our arms, making ready to engage. It was a false alarm.

Our fatigue parties were out for forage and we were busy cooking when the signal was given on the 25th of July. The two rear companies moved to the heights, the rest of the regiment to the alarm post, where we had work enough upon our arrival. The French were in great force, moving up the heights in solid column. We killed great numbers of them in their advance; but they still moved on. We were forced to give way and continued thus to retire, maintaining every height to the last, contesting every foot of ground. At length we were forced to the height where our old quarter-guard used to be posted. We maintained our position against them a considerable time, during which we had the mortification to see the French making merry in our camp, eating the dinner we had cooked for ourselves. What could we do? They were so much superior in numbers.

I have often admired the bravery of the French officers. This day, while I was in the rearguard, covering the retreat, about two dozen of us were pursued and molested by a company of the French. Out of breath and unable to run farther, we cried, 'Let us make a stand and get breath, else we will never reach the top.' 'Take your will,' returned the officers. Immediately we faced about the French halted; their officers pricked them on. We formed front across the road, and charged–the French officers in the rear urging their troops forward. All would not do; the men forced their officers fairly over the hill and ran. We had what we wished, an unmolested retreat, and moved slowly up the height. We were then joined by a brigade of Brunswickers,[4] gave three cheers and charged the French along the heights, keeping up our fire till dark. A part of the regiment made fires, while the remainder kept their ground upon the main height until about twelve o'clock. We then marched off towards the Black Forest, leaving our wounded, whose cries were piercing, but we could not help them. Numbers continued to follow us, crawling on their hands and knees, filling the air with their groans. Many, who could not do so, held out their hands, supplicating to be taken with us. We tore ourselves away, and hurried to get out of sight. We could not bear it.

The roads were very bad, the rain continued to pour and we made but little way. At daybreak we formed on the outside of Maya and got orders to cook, but scarce had we begun when the French made their appearance. We immediately moved on to a stronger height on the opposite side and encamped. Here we got three days allowance of beef and bread served out to each man and an allowance of liquor. As soon as cooking was over we marched on to the Black Forest and never halted until two o'clock in the morning. The night was dark and stormy. The wounded officers were carried in blankets on the shoulders of the men. The wounded soldiers who had been enabled still to keep up with us made the heart bleed at their cries; while the forcing up of the baggage caused such a noise that the whole was a scene of misery and confusion. We halted to allow the baggage to get forward.

Shortly after daylight the French advance came up with our rearguard, consisting of a brigade of Portuguese, which continued to skirmish all the way through the forest. We lost a great number of men in this forest, unable to

keep up through illness and fatigue and not a few from
the effects of liquor. It was found necessary to stave the
stores of liquor; and the men were carrying it away in
their bonnets. Many were intoxicated and carried upon
the shoulders of their comrades.

We at length got out of the forest and encamped.
Picquets were posted and we began to cook; but we had
scarcely commenced when the French were again upon
us. The camp was moved and we marched until two
hours after dark. We were then drawn up in column
and lay down on the bare ground until next morning.
The French moved about two miles and then turned off
on their left towards Pamplona, thinking there was
nothing to stop them. We remained here until morning.

Day was scarce broke when we heard three guns
fire towards our right. All were under arms in a moment;
and we stood in this situation a considerable time. The
noise of artillery and musketry was incessant on our
right; but, towards the afternoon, the firing ceased and
the French were forced from the heights opposite Pamplona. After Lord Wellington had defeated them, they
retreated by our right.

We got orders to occupy a height in the wood. Two
companies were sent, at extended order, down the wood,
where we were not long before the enemy began to
appear; and the firing commenced with their skirmishers.
After doing our utmost for some time, we were forced
to retire to the top of the height, and, when we arrived
upon it, they were so numerous it was vain to contend.
We gave them two or three volleys and retired through
a small village, they following close in the rear. Then
we drew up along the side of a strong rock, close by the
main road, determined to defend it to the last. Lord

Wellington sent a division to our assistance. The enemy, seeing them approach, drew up and continued to annoy us for some time; then fell back upon the village and encamped. There were some fine fields of grain here, which they set fire to. We lay down fatigued and weary, having been constantly engaged almost the whole afternoon.

Next morning, the 5th of August the enemy began to retire; we following close at their heels through the Black Forest. They retired back into France. We halted upon our old camp ground, for the space of half an hour and then returned to our old quarters at Maya. We were very melancholy, the whole bringing to our minds the time when we last left it and our wounded and dying comrades.

After encamping on a height on the other side for two or three days, we were marched round to the heights of Roncesvalles, where we encamped, relieving a brigade of the 7th division. We lay here for a considerable time, working like galley slaves from morning till evening in building batteries and block-houses. All the time I had been a soldier my labour could not stand in the least comparison with my fatigues at this time.

Orders were given that the heights should be kept by the 3rd and 4th division, week about, alternately. We retired, moving down, and encamped on the other side of the village.

A short time afterwards we got orders for duty on the heights on the opposite side, of which we were glad, thinking that the work would not be so severe. But we were disagreeably undeceived. Our labour was incessant; every day we were either on guard or on fatigue. All the time we remained here we were not a night in bed out of two. Besides, the weather was dreadful; we had always either snow or hail, the hail often as large as nuts. We were forced to put our knapsacks on our heads to protect us from its violence. The mules, at these times, used to run crying up and down, hurt by the stones. The frost was most severe, accompanied by high winds. Often, for whole days and nights, we could not get a tent to stand. Many of us were frost-bitten and others were found dead at their posts. At this time I cursed my hard fate, and groaned over my folly. Frequently have I been awakened through the night by the sobs of those around me in the tent; more especially by the young soldiers, who had not been long from their mothers' fire-sides. They often spent the darkness of the night in tears. The weather was so dreadful, the 92nd regiment got grey trousers served out to them. They could not live with their kilts; the cold would have killed them.

In about two days after we went down to the valley, the day being good, the French came down from the heights nearest France. General Stewart[5] being there at the same time with our advanced post, and seeing their manœuvres, ordered us to advance towards them. We soon beat them back and retired to our post. A few days afterwards the weather was so very bad that great numbers of the men fell sick. We were then forced to leave the heights and encamp in the valley, leaving strong picquets in the block-houses on the main pass, which were relieved daily. Fatigue parties were sent up to work, nevertheless, every day the weather would permit. At this time we buried two guns of Captain Mitchell's brigade of artillery, which displeased him much. Through intercession, General Stewart ordered up a fatigue party to raise them again. We were covered by the picquets, and, with great difficulty, at length got them raised and brought down to the valley. Each man on fatigue got an extra allowance of grog, the only welcome recompence.

We lay here for some time, frequently attacked in the block-houses by the French, and at length received orders to leave our purgatory in the heights and move round towards Maya. We marched that whole afternoon and all night until next morning, when the whole army formed on the other side of Maya. We were appointed the brigade of reserve, being far in the rear, and very much fatigued. An attack was begun almost as soon as we arrived. We moved towards the enemy's works which were very strong, but we forced them out, then moved round to our own right, the remainder of the army pursuing them. Their camp-ground, which was hutted like a little town, was occupied by us during the night.

November 10.—We, next morning, continued to move to our own right, until we came to a village called Cambo, on the outside of which the enemy had batteries planted, and strong works. We kept up a severe fire for some time, but could not storm their works on account of the depth of the entrenchments. They found out that the Spanish troops under Morillo[6] were fording the river on their right. We retired back into camp and lay there two days. The weather was so bad we could not move out.

In the afternoon they blew up the bridge over the Nive and retired out of the town. We then marched into it and were cantoned, and lay there for a considerable time, the French on one side and we on the other, our sentinel and their's, on the bridge, not five yards asunder. The night before we crossed the French came down to the banks of the river with their music and gave us a tune or two. We thought to change their tune before next night. We were then to be all under arms at a minute's notice.

About nine o'clock the whole of our inlying picquets were called to cover a party of sappers and miners in raising a battery to cover our fording ground; and the sentinel on the broken bridge received orders to shoot the French sentinel on the first gun for alarm being fired. Both were walking from one parapet to another, the Frenchman unconscious of any unusual danger, the English sentinel listening and often looking to the victim, his heart revolting from the deed he dared not disobey. The match touched the signal gun; next moment the French sentinel fell into the river, pierced by a ball.

As soon as the sappers and miners had constructed the battery, we moved back into the town and remained until an hour before day. We were drawn up on our fording ground; orders were given that not a man should speak above his breath. The whole being prepared, the word was given to pass the river when three guns were fired on our left. Our right wing was sent out to cover the fording. The left forded the river; but we had not reached the opposite bank when we received a volley from the enemy's picquets. We gave three cheers, splashed through the water; they retired and we pursued them. The regiment formed upon the top of the height, sending out two companies to follow the enemy close; but they never came up with them.

All the night of the 11th of December we lay in camp upon the face of a height, near the Spaniards. In the afternoon of the 12th we received orders to move round towards Bayonne where we were quartered along the main road. There we remained a few days until we received orders to march to our own right to assist a Spanish force, who were engaged with superior numbers. We set off by daylight in the morning of the 13th towards them and were moving on when General Hill sent an aide-de-camp after us, saying, 'That is not the direction—follow me'. We put to the right about, to the main road towards Bayonne. We soon came to the scene of action and were immediately engaged. We had continued firing, without intermission, for five hours, advancing and retreating, and lost a great number of men, but could not gain a bit of ground. Towards evening we were relieved by a brigade which belonged to another division. As many of us as could be collected were drawn up. General Hill gave us great praise for our behaviour this day and ordered an extra allowance of liquor to each man. We were marched back to our old quarters along the roadside.

The day's service had been very severe, but now I took it with the coolest indifference. I felt no alarm; it was all of course. I began to think my body charmed. My mind had come to that pass; I took everything as it came without a thought. If I was at ease, with plenty, I was happy; if in the midst of the enemy's fire, or of the greatest privations, I was not concerned. I had been in so many changes of plenty and want, ease and danger, they had ceased to be anticipated either with joy or fear.[7]

We lay upon the roadside for two or three days, having two companies three leagues to the rear, carrying the wounded to the hospital. We were next cantoned three leagues above Bayonne, along the side of the river. We had strong picquets planted along the banks. The

French were cantoned upon the other side. Never a night passed that we were not molested by boats passing up and down the river, with provisions and necessaries to the town. Our orders were to turn out and keep up a constant fire upon them while passing. We had two grasshopper guns planted upon the side of the river, by means of which we one night sunk a boat loaded with clothing for the army, setting it on fire with red-hot shot.[8]

Next day we were encamped in the rear of the town, being relieved by a brigade of Portuguese. We remained in camp two or three days, expecting to be attacked, the enemy having crossed above us on the river. We posted picquets in the town, near our camp. At length, receiving orders to march, we moved on, until we came to a river on our right, which ran very swift. Part of the regiment having crossed, we got orders to come to the right-about and were marched back to our old camp ground. Next morning we received orders to take another road towards Salvatierra where we encamped that night and remained until the whole army assembled the following day.

About two o'clock in the afternoon we were under arms and moved towards the river, covered by a brigade of artillery. We forded and continued to skirmish alongst the heights until the town was taken. We lost only one man during the whole time. We encamped upon the other side of the town and next morning followed the line of march until we came before a town called Garris. We had severe fighting before we got into it. We were led on by an aide-de-camp. The contest lasted until after dark. We planted picquets in different streets of the town; the enemy did the same in others. Different patrols were sent out during the night, but the French were always found on the alert. They retired before daylight and we marched into the town, with our music at the head of the regiments. The town appeared then quite desolate, not worth twopence; but we were not three days in it until the French inhabitants came back, opened their shops and houses, and it became a fine lively place. There was a good deal of plundering the first night, for the soldiers, going into the houses and finding no person within, helped themselves. The people have a way of keeping their fowls in cans full of grease, about the size of a hen. This we found out by accident, for, wanting some grease to fry in cooking, we took one of these cans and cut out the fowl. We commenced a search for the grease cans and were very successful. The fowls were excellent. We lay here a considerable time, then were marched towards Toulouse, and halted at a village four leagues from it, with orders to turn out on a moment's notice. We were drawn out at twelve o'clock at night and marched close up to the town, designing to throw a bridge over the river, but it ran so swift that we failed in our attempt. We then kindled fires in all quarters and returned to the village. Next morning we marched round towards the main road to Toulouse and were cantoned along the road. We lay here for some time, and were every morning under arms an hour before day.

At length, on the 10th of April, we received orders to attack Toulouse and moved on by another road, on the opposite side from the one we had lain upon. We were drawn up in column, in rear of a house, and remained there for some time, sending out the flank companies to skirmish and, at length, forced the enemy back upon their works. The contest now began to be more severe. A brigade of guns coming up, played upon their works for some time, and then retired, night coming on. We were posted in the different streets of the suburbs to watch the enemy's motions. At last we got our allowance of liquor served out and retired to our cantonment.

I shall ever remember an adventure that happened to me towards the afternoon. We were in extended order, firing and retiring. I had just risen to run behind my file when a spent shot struck me on the groin and took the breath from me. 'God receive my soul!' I said, and sat down resigned. The French were advancing fast. I laid my musket down and gasped for breath. I was sick and put my canteen to my head, but could not taste the water. However, I washed my mouth and grew less faint. I looked to my thigh and, seeing no blood, took resolution to put my hand to the part to feel the wound. My hand was unstained by blood; but the part was so painful that I could not touch it. At this moment of helplessness the French came up. One of them made a charge at me as I sat pale as death. In another moment I would have been transfixed had not his next man forced the point past me. 'Do not touch the good Scot,' said he, and then, addressing himself to me, added, 'Do you remember me?' I had not recovered my breath sufficiently to speak distinctly. I answered, 'No.' 'I saw you at Sobral,' he replied. Immediately I recognized him to be a soldier whose life I had saved from a Portuguese, who was going to kill him as he lay wounded. 'Yes, I know you,' I replied. 'God bless you!' cried he and, giving me a pancake out of his hat, moved on with his fellows, the rear of whom took my knapsack and left me lying. I had fallen down for greater security. I soon recovered so far as to walk, though with pain, and joined the regiment next advance.

We were quartered in wine stores, where we lay for a considerable time, sending out a regiment each night on duty. The 71st happened to be the regiment on duty on the night in which the French evacuated Toulouse. We immediately gave notice and marched into the town; halted half an hour until the cavalry passed through it, and then moved on after them. We fell in with a number of the enemy's sick and wounded, whom we sent back to the town. We halted at Villafranca and were cantoned. Soult lay in a town on the heights in front, about one league and a half from us.

We remained here two or three days, when we were all turned out, cavalry and artillery, the French being under arms. Three guns were fired. The French did not seem inclined to attack us. We were encamped again. In the course of the day, flags of truce were passing between the armies. At length, General Soult came in his carriage, guarded by a squadron of his cavalry. We then got word that Bonaparte was deposed, and we were soon to have peace. Joy beamed on every face, and made every tongue eloquent. We sung and drank that whole night and talked of home. Next morning, falling back to Toulouse, we were cantoned there and lay for a long time, looking anxiously for orders to embark for England. At length we marched to Bordeaux, were reviewed by Lord Wellington and embarked for Ireland.

NOTES

[1] On Cadogan's death, Major Charles Cotter took command of the regiment.

[2] The 71st suffered more heavily than any other regiment at Vitoria. In addition to Colonel Cadogan they lost fourteen other officers killed or wounded and 301 other ranks.

[3] This is, presumably, a misprint for 'roads and earthworks' The author disappeared before the book was published and a civilian proof-reader may have supposed 'rows and rain-works' to be military expressions.

[4] The Brunswick Oels Jägers, organized in England in 1809 around a nucleus of refugees from North Germany who had fought under George III's nephew, Frederick William, Duke of Brunswick, against Jerome Bonaparte. The men, Poles, Danes, Swiss, Dutch and Croats as well as Germans, were largely recruited in English prison camps and offered their release from confinement in exchange for service against Napoleon.

[5] Lieutenant-General William Stewart (1774–1827), commander of the 2nd Division. He was known as 'auld grog Willie' because of the extra allowances of rum which he authorized—and for which Wellington made him pay out of his own pocket.

[6] Pablo Morillo, Count of Cartagena (1777–1832).

[7] During the fighting on 13th December, Colonel Peacock, who had returned to command the regiment after Cadogan's death, had pusillanimously marched his men out of the line. Realizing that he was acting without orders, his second-in-command, Major Macdonald, over-ruled him and marched the regiment back again. Peacock was later found among the baggage by Wellington. He was relieved of his command.

[8] Grasshopper guns were light mobile guns, mounted on an unusual type of carriage with a third wheel at the end of the trail so as to make them manœuvreable without a linker. They were probably three-pounders and designed

primarily for colonial campaigns where heavier guns would have been an embarrassment. It is likely that some of the earliest made guns (which were first employed in 1813 in the Pyrenees) consisted of this type of piece. It is doubtful, however, that the author is correct in saying the boat was set alight by red-hot shot. Using red-hot shot was a highly technical business, employed mainly at sieges and for coast defence against wooden ships. Perhaps the shot hit a cooking-stove or lamp, or munitions in the cargo, and set the boat alight.

8

Waterloo
1815

The 71st arrived back in Cork in June, 1814. The author —one of the only 75 survivors of the original 650 men who had sailed to Portugal in 1810—had now been seven years and eleven months in the Army and hoped for his discharge. But the seven years for which he had enlisted were counted from his eighteenth birthday, so, as he had been sixteen at the time of his enlistment, he found he had another thirteen months to serve.

Upon our arrival at Cork we were marched to Limerick and lay there a long time; then got the route for Cork to embark for America. I lamented my becoming a soldier, at this time, more than I had done on the retreat or upon the Pyrenees. To be so near home and almost free, and yet to be sent across the Atlantic, was very galling. I knew not what to do. I kept my honour and embarked. What vexed me was some being discharged who had not been so long soldiers as I had been; only they were above eighteen when they enlisted.

We lay on board six weeks before setting sail. When on our way, a schooner fired a gun and brought us to and gave us orders for Deal.[1] My heart bounded with joy. Freedom, freedom! I would not have taken a thousand pounds to stay. I would have left the army without a shirt. I was oppressed all the time I was on board; my mind dwelt on nothing but home. If anyone asked a question or spoke to me, I was so absent that I seldom answered to the point. After the ship was put about for England, a load was taken from my mind and I became more happy. We landed all our heavy baggage at Deal, then sailed round to Gravesend and disembarked. We lay there only one afternoon, then were put on board the smacks and were landed at Antwerp.

Next morning we were marched to Leuze, where we lay, quartered in the different villages around, until the 16th of June, 1815.² We used to be drilled every day. We were going out for a field-day on the 16th when we were ordered back and formed on one side of the village. We stopped here a short time; then were sent to quarters to pack up every thing and march. We immediately marched off towards the French frontier. We had a very severe march of sixteen miles, expecting to halt and be quartered in every town through which we passed. We knew not where we were marching. About one o'clock in the morning we were halted in a village. A brigade of Brunswickers marching out, we took their quarters, hungry and weary.

Next morning, the 17th, we got our allowance of liquor and moved on until the heat of the day when we encamped, and our baggage was ordered to take the high road to Brussels. We sent out fatigue parties for water, and set a-cooking. Our fires were not well kindled when we got orders to fall in and move on along the high road towards Waterloo. The whole length of the road was very much crowded by artillery and ammunition carts, all advancing towards Waterloo. The troops were much embarrassed in marching, the roads were so crowded. As soon as we arrived on the ground, we formed in column. The rain began to pour. The firing had never ceased all yesterday and today at a distance. We encamped and began to cook, when the enemy came in sight and again spoiled our cooking. We advanced towards them. When we reached the height they retired, which caused the whole army to get under arms and move to their positions. Night coming on, we stood under arms for some time. The army then retired to their own rear and lay down under arms, leaving the 71st in advance. During the whole night the rain never ceased. Two hours after daybreak General Hill came down, taking away the left sub-division of the 10th company to cover his recognisance. Shortly afterwards we got half an allowance of liquor, which was the most welcome thing I ever received. I was so stiff and sore from the rain I could not move with freedom for some time. A little afterwards, the weather clearing up, we began to clean our arms and prepare for action. The whole of the opposite heights were covered by the enemy.

A young lad who had joined but a short time before said to me, while we were cleaning: 'Tom, you are an old soldier, and have escaped often, and have every chance to escape this time also. I am sure I am to fall.' 'Nonsense, be not gloomy.' 'I am certain,' he said. 'All I ask is that you will tell my parents when you get home that I ask God's pardon for the evil I have done and the grief I have given them. Be sure to tell I died praying for their blessing and pardon.' I grew dull myself, but gave him all the heart I could. He only shook his head. I could say nothing to alter his belief.

The artillery had been tearing away since daybreak in different parts of the line. About twelve o'clock we received orders to fall in for attack. We then marched up to our position, where we lay on the face of a brae, covering a brigade of guns. We were so overcome by the fatigue of the two days' march that, scarce had we lain down, until many of us fell asleep. I slept sound for some time while the cannonballs, plunging in amongst us, killed a great many. I was suddenly awakened. A ball struck the ground a little below me, turned me heels-over-head, broke my musket in pieces and killed a lad at my side. I was stunned and confused and knew not whether I was wounded or not. I felt a numbness in my arm for some time.

We lay thus, about an hour and a half, under a dreadful fire, which cost us about 60 men, while we had never fired a shot. The balls were falling thick amongst us. The young man I lately spoke of lost his legs by a shot at this time. They were cut very close; he soon bled to death. 'Tom,' he said, 'remember your charge: my mother wept sore when my brother died in her arms. Do not tell her all how I died; if she saw me thus, it would break her heart. Farewell, God bless my parents!' He said no more, his lips quivered and he ceased to breathe.

About two o'clock a squadron of lancers came down, hurraying, to charge the brigade of guns. They knew not what was in the rear. General Barnes[3] gave the word, 'Form square'. In a moment the whole brigade were on their feet, ready to receive the enemy. The General said, 'Seventy-first, I have often heard of your bravery, I hope it will not be worse than it has been today.' Down they came upon our square. We soon put them to the right-about.

Shortly after, we received orders to move to the heights. Onwards we marched and stood for a short time in square, receiving cavalry every now and then. The noise and smoke were dreadful. At this time I could see but a very little way from me, but all around the wounded and slain lay very thick. We then moved on in column for a considerable way and formed line, gave three cheers, fired a few volleys, charged the enemy and drove them back.

At this moment a squadron of cavalry rode furiously down upon our line. Scarce had we time to form. The square was only complete in front when they were upon the points of our bayonets. Many of our men were out of place. There was a good deal of jostling, for a minute or two, and a good deal of laughing. Our quartermaster lost his bonnet in riding into the square; got it up, put it on, back foremost, and wore it thus all day. Not a moment had we to regard our dress. A French General lay dead in the square; he had a number of ornaments upon his breast. Our men fell to plucking them off, pushing each other as they passed, and snatching at them.

We stood in square for some time, whilst the 13th dragoons and a squadron of French dragoons were engaged. The 13th dragoons retiring to the rear of our column, we gave the French a volley, which put them to the right-about; then the 13th at them again. They did this for some time; we cheering the 13th, and feeling every blow they received. When a Frenchman fell we shouted; and when one of the 13th, we groaned. We wished to join them but were forced to stand in square.

The whole army retired to the heights in the rear, the French closely pursuing to our formation, where we stood, four deep, for a considerable time. As we fell back, a shot cut the straps of the knapsack of one near me; it fell and was rolling away. He snatched it up, saying, 'I am not to lose you that way; you are all I have in the world,' tied it on the best manner he could and marched on.

Lord Wellington came riding up.[4] We formed square, with him in our centre, to receive cavalry.[5] Shortly the whole army received orders to advance. We moved forwards in two columns, four deep, the French retiring at the same time. We were charged several times in our advance. This was our last effort; nothing could impede us. The whole of the enemy retired, leaving their guns and ammunition and every other thing behind. We moved on towards a village and charged right through, killing great numbers, the village was so crowded. We then formed on the other side of it and lay down under the canopy of heaven, hungry and wearied to death. We had been oppressed all day by the weight of our blankets and greatcoats which were drenched with rain and lay upon our shoulders like logs of wood.

Scarce was my body stretched upon the ground when sleep closed my eyes. Next morning when I awoke I was quite stupid. The whole night my mind had been harassed by dreams. I was fighting and charging, re-acting the scenes of the day, which were strangely jumbled with the scenes I had been in before. I rose up and looked around, and began to recollect. The events of the 18th came before me, one by one; still they were confused, the whole appearing as an unpleasant dream. My comrades began to awake and talk of it; then the events were embodied as realities. Many an action had I been in wherein the individual exertions of our regiment had been much greater and our fighting more severe; but never had I been where the firing was so dreadful and the noise so great. When I looked over the field of battle it was covered and heaped in many places, figures moving up and down upon it. The wounded crawling along the rows of the dead was a horrible spectacle; yet I looked on with less concern, I must say, at the moment, than I have felt at an accident, when in quarters. I have been sad at the burial of a comrade who died of sickness in the hospital and followed him almost in tears; yet have I seen, after a battle, fifty men put into the same trench, and comrades amongst them, almost with indifference. I looked over the field of Waterloo as a matter of course, a matter of small concern.[6]

In the morning we got half an allowance of liquor and remained here until midday, under arms; then received orders to cook. When cooking was over, we marched on towards France. Nothing particular happened before reaching Paris, where we lay in the lines until the French capitulated. We had our posts planted at each side of the city. The French troops retired and we got under arms and marched towards the gates. We had a cannon on each side of the gate, and gunners with lighted matches standing by them. We marched into the city, passed Lord Wellington, who stood at the gates, and were encamped on the main road in the Tuilleries, where we remained all the time we were here.

In marching through the city, a lad dressed as a Frenchman was looking up the companies very anxiously. One of our men said, 'Knock the French fellow down'. 'Dinna be sae fast, man,' said he. We stared to hear broad Scotch in Paris at this time. 'I am looking for my cousin,' he added, naming him; but he had been left behind, wounded.

When we were in camp before the Tuilleries, the first day, two girls were looking very eagerly up and down the regiment, when we were on parade. 'Do you wish a careless husband, my dear?' said one of our lads. 'May be; will you be't?' said a Glasgow voice. 'Where the devil do you come from?' said the rough fellow. 'We're Paisley lasses; this is our regiment. We want to see if there's ony body here we ken.' The soldier, who was a Glasgow lad, could not speak. There is a music in our native tongue, in a foreign land where it is not to be looked for, that often melts the heart when we hear it unexpectedly. These two girls had found their way from Paisley to Paris, and were working at tambouring, and did very well.[7]

We lay three months in Paris. All that time I saw very little of it. I did not care to ask leave from the camp. At length we were marched to Flanders, to winter quarters, and I got my discharge. I left my comrades with regret, but the service with joy. I came down to the coast to embark, with light steps and a joyful heart, singing, 'When wild war's deadly blast was blawn'. I was poor as poor could be; but I had hope before me, and pleasing dreams of home. I had saved nothing this campaign; and the money I had before was all gone. Government found me the means of getting to Edinburgh. Hope and joy were my companion until I entered the Firth. I was on deck; the morning began to dawn; the shores of Lothian began to rise out of the mist. 'There is the land of cakes,' said the captain. A sigh escaped me; recollections crowded upon me, painful recollections. I went below to conceal my feelings and never came up until the vessel was in the harbour. I ran from her and hid myself in a public house. All the time I had been away was forgot. I felt as if I had been in Leith the day before. I was so foolish as to think I would be known and laughed at. In about half an hour I reasoned myself out of my foolish notions; but I could not bring myself to go up the Walk to Edinburgh. I went by the Easter Road. Everything was strange to me, so many alterations had taken place; yet I was afraid to look any person in the face lest he should recognize me. I was suffering as keenly, at this moment, as when I went away. I felt my face burning with shame. At length I reached the door of the last house I had been in before leaving Edinburgh. I had not power to knock; happy was it for me that I did not. A young girl came into the stair. I asked her if Mrs——lived there. 'No,' she said, 'she had flitted long ago.' 'Where does she live?' 'I do not know.' Where to go I knew not. I came down stairs and recognized a sign which had been in the same place before I went away. In I went, and inquired. The landlord knew me. 'Tom,' said he, 'Are you come back safe? Poor fellow! Give me your hand.' 'Does my mother live?' 'Yes, yes; come in, and I will send for her, not to let the surprise be too great.' Away he went. I could not remain, but followed him and, the next minute, I was in the arms of my mother.

The author completed the manuscript of this book in May, 1818, and sent it to a friend in the hope that it might be published. His mother had then died and he was living with his married sister to whom he felt himself to be a burden. 'I cannot even get labouring work,' he wrote to his friend from Edinburgh. 'I would be useful but can get nothing to do . . . I will go to South America.

Maria de Parides will put me in a way to do for myself,
and be a burden to no one. Or, I shall go to Spain and
live in Bejar. Farewell, John! This manuscript is all I
have to leave you. It is yours. Do with it as you think
proper. If I succeed in the South, I will return and lay my
bones besides my parents; if not, I will never come back
... I wish I was a soldier again.'

He disappeared before the book was published and
was last seen working as a road mender 'with a number
of other poor labourers thrown out of general employment'.

NOTES

[1] Unfavourable winds prevented the 71st from crossing the
Atlantic to join the British army fighting the United States;
and Napoleon's escape from Elba eventually led to their
being sent to the Continent once more.

[2] At Leuze they joined the 52nd, the Second Battalion of the
95th and two companies of the 3rd Battalion of the 95th to
form the light brigade under Major-General Frederick Adam.
This brigade was in General Clinton's division which was in
Lord Hill's Corps.

[3] Major-General Sir Edward Barnes (1776–1838), the Adjutant-
General. He was later severely wounded.

[4] Wellington had, in fact, been created Marquess of Douro and
Duke of Wellington on 3 May, 1814.

[5] This was one of seven times that the 71st formed square to
repulse cavalry charges at Waterloo.

[6] The losses of the 71st that day, killed and wounded, were
sixteen officers, eleven sergeants and 187 rank and file.

[7] Tambour-work is embroidery done with a special needle on
material stitched on a circular frame formed of one hoop
fitted inside another.

E

APPENDIX

CHANGES IN TITLES OF REGIMENTS MENTIONED IN THE TEXT

Original number until 1881	County affiliation or other title in 1806	Title in 1881
1st	The Royal Regiment of Foot	The Lothian Regiment (Royal Scots)
4th	The King's Own Regiment	The King's Own (Royal Lancaster Regiment)
9th	9th (East Norfolk) Regiment of Foot	The Norfolk Regiment
13th	13th (1st Somersetshire) Regiment of Foot	The Prince Albert's (Somerset Light Infantry)
14th	14th (Bedfordshire) Regiment of Foot	The Prince of Wales's Own (West Yorkshire Regiment)
24th	24th (2nd Warwickshire) Regiment of Foot	The South Wales Borderers
26th	26th Cameronian Regiment	26th Cameronian Regiment
29th	29th (Worcestershire) Regiment of Foot	The Worcestershire Regiment

Title in 1957	Present Title
The Royal Scots (The Royal Regiment)	The Royal Scots (The Royal Regiment)
The King's Own Royal Regiment (Lancaster)	The King's Own Royal Border Regiment [Amalgamated with 34th and 55th]
The Royal Norfolk Regiment	The Royal Anglian Regiment [Amalgamated with 10th, 12th, 16th, 17th, 44th, 48th, 56th and 58th]
The Somerset Light Infantry (Prince Albert's)	The Light Infantry [Amalgamated with 32nd, 46th, 51st, 53rd, 68th, 85th, 105th and 106th]
The West Yorkshire Regiment (The Prince of Wales's Own)	The Prince of Wales's Own Regiment of Yorkshire [Amalgamated with 15th]
The South Wales Borderers	The Royal Regiment of Wales [Amalgamated with 41st]
The Cameronians (Scottish Rifles)	The Cameronians (Scottish Rifles) [Amalgamated with 90th]
The Worcestershire Regiment	The Worcestershire and Sherwood Foresters Regiment [Amalgamated with 36th, 45th and 95th]

Original number until 1881	County affiliation or other title in 1806	Title in 1881
36th	36th (Herefordshire) Regiment of Foot	The Worcestershire Regiment
38th	38th (1st Staffordshire) Regiment of Foot	The South Staffordshire Regiment
40th	40th (2nd Somersetshire) Regiment of Foot	The South Lancashire Regiment (The Prince of Wales's Volunteers)
42nd	42nd (The Royal Highland) Regiment of Foot	The Black Watch (Royal Highlanders)
50th	50th (West Kent) Regiment of Foot	The Queen's Own (Royal West Kent) Regiment
51st	51st (2nd Yorkshire West Riding) Regiment of Foot	The King's Own Yorkshire Light Infantry
59th	59th (2nd Nottinghamshire) Regiment of Foot	The East Lancashire Regiment

Title in 1957	Present Title
The Worcestershire Regiment	The Worcestershire and Sherwood Forester Regiment [Amalgamated with 29th, 45th and 95th]
The South Staffordshire Regiment	The Staffordshire Regiment (The Prince of Wales's) [Amalgamated with 64th, 80th and 98th]
The Lancashire Regiment (The Prince of Wales's Volunteers)	The Queen's Lancashire Regiment [Amalgamated with 30th, 47th, 59th, 81st and 82nd]
The Black Watch (Royal Highland Regiment)	The Black Watch (Royal Highland Regiment) [Amalgamated with 73rd]
The Queen's Own (Royal West Kent) Regiment	The Queen's Regiment [Amalgamated with 2nd, 3rd, 31st, 35th, 57th, 70th, 77th, 97th and 107th]
The King's Own Yorkshire Light Infantry	The Light Infantry [Amalgamated with 13th, 32nd, 46th, 53rd, 68th, 85th, 105th and 106th]
The Lancashire Regiment (Prince of Wales's Volunteers)	The Queen's Lancashire Regiment [Amalgamated with 30th, 40th, 47th, 81st and 82nd]

Original number until 1881	County affiliation or other title in 1806	Title in 1881
60th	60th (Royal American) Regiment of Foot	The King's Royal Rifle Corps
68th	68th (Durham) Regiment of Foot	The Durham Light Infantry
71st	71st (Highland) Regiment of Foot	The Highland Light Infantry
76th	76th (Hindoostan) Regiment of Foot	The Duke of Wellington's Regiment (West Riding)
79th	79th Regiment of Foot (Cameronian High-landers)	The Queen's Own Cameron Highlanders
81st	81st Regiment of Foot	The Loyal North Lancashire Regiment
85th	85th (Bucks Volunteers) Regiment of Foot	85th (The King's Light Infantry) Regiment

Title in 1957	Present Title
2nd Green Jackets, The King's Royal Rifle Corps	The Royal Green Jackets [Amalgamated with 43rd, 52nd and Rifle Brigade]
The Durham Light Infantry	The Light Infantry [Amalgamated with 13th, 32nd, 46th, 51st, 53rd, 85th, 105th and 106th]
The Highland Light Infantry	The Royal Highland Fusiliers (Princess Margaret's Own Glasgow and Ayrshire Regiment) [Amalgamated with 21st and 74th]
The Duke of Wellington's Regiment (West Riding)	The Duke of Wellington's Regiment (West Riding) [Amalgamated with 33rd]
The Queen's Own Cameron Highlanders	Queen's Own Highlanders (Seaforth and Camerons) [Amalgamated with 72nd and 78th]
The Loyal Regiment (North Lancashire)	The Queen's Lancashire Regiment [Amalgamated with 30th, 40th, 47th, 59th and 82nd]
The King's Shropshire Light Infantry	The Light Infantry [Amalgamated with 13th, 32nd, 46th, 51st, 53rd, 68th, 105th and 106th]

Original number until 1881	County affiliation or other title in 1806	Title in 1881
87th	87th (The Prince of Wales's Irish) Regiment of Foot	Princess Victoria's (The Royal Irish Fusiliers)
88th	88th (Connaught Rangers) Regiment of Foot	The Connaught Rangers
92nd	92nd (Highland) Regiment of Foot	The Gordon Highlanders
95th	The 95th Regiment became the Rifle Brigade in 1815 when its number was re-allotted to an ordinary line battalion	The Sherwood Foresters (Derbyshire Regiment)

Title in 1957	Present Title
The Royal Irish Fusiliers (Princess Victoria's)	The Royal Irish Rangers [Amalgamated with 83rd]
Disbanded (1922)	Disbanded (1922)
The Gordon Highlanders	The Gordon Highlanders [Amalgamated with 75th]
The Sherwood Foresters (Nottinghamshire and Derbyshire Regiment)	The Worcestershire and Sherwood Foresters Regiment [Amalgamated with 29th, 36th, and 45th]

The Windrush Press

MILITARY HISTORY BOOKS

THE LETTERS OF PRIVATE WHEELER 1809–1828

An eyewitness account of the Battle of Waterloo
Edited and with a foreword by B. H. Liddell Hart
'*Vivid images – of people, landscape, events – flow from his
pen . . . one of military history's great originals*'
John Keegan
Paperback £9.99

THE DIARY OF A NAPOLEONIC FOOT SOLDIER
Jakob Walter

A conscript in the *Grande Armée's* account of the long march
home on the retreat from Moscow
Edited and Introduced by Mark Raeff
Paperback £9.99 Illustrated

THE RECOLLECTIONS OF RIFLEMAN HARRIS

One of the most popular military books of all time.
Edited and Introduced by Christopher Hibbert
'*Describing narrow squeaks and terrible deprivations, Harris's account
of fortitude and resilience in Spain still bristles with a freshness and an
invigorating spikiness.*'
Scotland on Sunday
'*An ordinary soldier's memoirs are rare but precious. Harris's are a
most vivid record of the war in Spain and Portugal against Napoleon,
the same campaign as featured in the recent TV drama series, 'Sharpe'.*'
The Mail on Sunday
Paperback £9.99